CREATIVE PLANNING IN THE EYFS

Spring

Lucy Peet

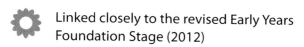

- Linked closely to the revised Early Years Foundation Stage (2012)

- Six weeks of differentiated planning

- Coverage across the 7 areas and 17 aspects of learning

- Activities based upon: Playing and Exploring; Active Learning; Creating and Thinking Critically

- Guidance on assessing characterisitics of learning

Published 2012 by Featherstone Education
Bloomsbury Publishing Plc
50 Bedford Square, London, WC1B 3DP
www.bloomsbury.com

ISBN 978-1-4081-7394-7

Text © Lucy Peet 2012
Design © Lynda Murray
Photographs © Shutterstock

Printed in Great Britain by Latimer Trend & Company Ltd

10 9 8 7 6 5 4 3 2 1

This book is produced using paper that is made from wood grown in
managed, sustainable forests. It is natural, renewable and recyclable.
The logging and manufacturing processes conform to the environmental
regulations of the country of origin.

To see our full range of titles visit www.bloomsbury.com

Contents

Introduction

About the series

This book is part of a series written for all who work with children in the Foundation Stage (FS). Owing to the fun, practical nature of the activities it is suitable for a wide range of settings, including schools, pre-schools, childminders and nurseries. Given that all the activities are differentiated for children working towards the Early Learning Goals (ELGs) 'the knowledge, skills and understanding children should have at the end of the academic year in which they turn five' (p.2, 2012), it is particularly relevant to practitioners working with FS1, FS2 and mixed-age classes. However, with the increasing good practice of the FS extending into Year 1 and 2 this book is invaluable for teachers wishing to promote active learning and a creative curriculum with children up to the age of seven. Each activity links with the requirements and expectations of the National Curriculum, statutory for Key Stage 1 in England and Wales, and through observation it will also be possible to collect evidence for Assessing Pupils' Progress. The table below shows the corresponding year groups for children from Scotland and Northern Ireland.

 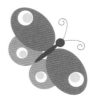

Year groups and corresponding ages:

Age	School year		
	England and Wales	**Scotland**	**Northern Ireland**
2 - 3	Foundation Stage		
3 - 4	FS1 (previously nursery)		P 1
4 - 5	FS2 (previously reception)	Primary 1	P 2
5 - 6	Year 1	Primary 2	P 3
6 - 7	Year 2	Primary 3	P 4

How this book is structured

Through the topic of autumn children will be involved in playing and exploring, active learning and creating and thinking critically: all key features of the revised Early Years Foundation Stage (EYFS) (2012). This book contains six weeks of planning – five weeks of detailed plans, with an activity designed for each specific area of learning, and a celebratory week of activity to share with parents and carers at the end covering the 'prime areas of learning'. Details are shown in the six week planning overview grid on page 62.

Activities are structured to build upon children's skills over the six weeks developing their experiences and abilities. For example, week 1 introduces a mathematical activity looking at shape and space, naming shapes and building curves, arches and bridges. This knowledge is extended in week 4 when the children learn how to make a 3D basket or box shape from a 2D net. Similarly, the introduction to information texts in week 3 (how to plant a bulb) is extended and consolidated in week 4 when the children make a simple information book about eggs and chicks.

Through this method of extending similar tasks at a later date children are able to consolidate their knowledge and practise their skills. The final week of celebration is an opportunity to share the topic with parents and carers.

Each activity is clearly structured, with suggestions for:

♦ Resources required with relevant storybook or non-fiction book suggestions to support the main idea

♦ Key vocabulary

♦ A simple 'what to do' explanation with ideas for both guided and independent activity

♦ Differentiation of the activity at three levels. Each activity is pitched at an average level of understanding in line with the expected level of the ELGs. There are also ideas to **support** children who are working at the emerging stage and to **extend** children who are exceeding the ELGs. This clear differentiation ensures that all children in the group are exploring new ideas and concepts at a level appropriate to their stage of development. The Statutory Framework for the Early Years Foundation Stage states that (p.11) 'Practitioners must indicate whether children are meeting expected levels of development, or if they are exceeding expected levels, or not yet reaching expected levels. This is the EYFS Profile. The extension activities in this book are planned in line with the National Curriculum, ensuring that the children are building a firm foundation for Years 1 and 2.

♦ How to extend the activity throughout the week, with suggestions on how to deliver the activity as a **guided** session and ideas on how to encourage the children to work **independently**. The Statutory Framework for the Early Years Foundation Stage recognises that there is an important balance between activities led by children and activities led or guided by adults. It is important that 'each area of learning and development must be implemented through planned, purposeful play and through a mix of adult-led and child-initiated activity' (p.6, 2012). Each activity in this book includes guidance for practitioners as to how this balance can be achieved.

♦ Ideas for interactive display within the setting

♦ Ideas for parents and carers to use at home

Parents and carers as partners

Parents and carers are crucial in developing and supporting children's learning. This is recognised in the revised EYFS, and a key recommendation from the Tickell Review is that (p.18) '...the Government increases the emphasis within the EYFS on the role of parents and carers as partners in their children's learning....'. Indeed, the *Statutory Framework for the Early Years Foundation Stage* (March 2012) states that (p.2) 'Good parenting and high quality early learning together provide the foundation children need to make the most of their abilities and talents as they grow up.' The planning in this book includes an entire week based around inviting parents and carers into the setting to share in their children's curiosity and enthusiasm for learning. There are examples of how parents and carers can extend the learning at home, and ideas for giving parents and carers the opportunity not only to see what activities their children have been involved in, but also for them to join in alongside their children and to be really 'hands on'! One of the features which the EYFS seeks to provide (p.2, 2012) is 'partnership working between practitioners and with parents and/or carers.' This book recognises this as a priority.

Outdoor learning

Most of the activities are more than suitable to be engaged with outdoors as well as in a classroom – indeed for some of the activities it is necessary to be outdoors! And for some very messy, noisy or extensive activities I would recommend setting up outdoors to save carpets and soft furnishings and to minimise disruption to the rest of the learning environment. Hardly any of the activities require the children to sit and write in a formal situation. Where there is a suggestion to record, it is done either by an adult on a flipchart, children on individual whiteboards or pictorially, or through ICT, for example by the children using a digital camera or making a sound recording.

The revised curriculum

It is four years since the EYFS was introduced to provide a framework for all children in early years settings. The Tickell Report (2011) was carried out as an evaluation of the EYFS on children's outcomes and on those people working in the early years. One of the recommendations from the Tickell Report (2011) was that…

> …the assessment at the end of the EYFS, the EYFS Profile, should be significantly slimmed down and made much more manageable, based upon [my] 17 proposed new early learning goals…

The themes, principles and commitments of the EYFS remain the same, however the fourth theme, Learning and development has changed. This is the focus of our *Creative Planning in the EYFS* series. The *Statutory Framework for the Early Years Foundation Stage* (March 2012) states that one of the overarching principles which should shape practice in early years settings (p.3) is that 'children develop and learn in different ways and at different rates'. This book shows how topic-based activities can be provided in an exciting and practical way whilst still offering opportunities for all children at three levels of differentiation.

The research studied for the Tickell Report (2011) focuses on the concept that some aspects of development and learning include developing abilities, enabling children to be successful in all areas. These are referred to as 'prime areas of learning' and development. Other areas of learning are more specific to areas of knowledge and skills, these are known as 'specific areas of learning and development'.

Prime areas of learning and development

1. Communication and language

2. Physical development

3. Personal, social and emotional development

Specific areas of learning and development

1. Literacy

2. Mathematics

3. Understanding the world

4. Expressive arts and design

The activities in this book are planned around the four specific areas of learning and development – Literacy (formerly Communication, Language and Literacy), Mathematics (formerly Problem Solving, Reasoning and Numeracy), Understanding the World (formerly Knowledge and Understanding of the World) and Expressive Arts and Design (formerly Creative Development). However, the three prime areas are also covered through discussion, speaking and listening, turn taking and involvement in each task. It is essential that the prime and specific areas are planned for and experienced at the same time. They are not to be experienced chronologically but as an interwoven fabric of early years provision, as 'all areas of learning and development are important and inter-connected' (p.4, 2012).

Development in the prime areas has been called by neuroscientists 'experience expectant learning'. This is where a child's brain is ready to respond to interaction and stimulus, developing connections. Development in the specific areas however, will only develop when the need occurs, and includes cultural concepts such as learning to read and write, understand numbers, the number system and maps. This has been referred to as 'experience dependent learning'. (Hall, 2005).

The revisions made in the EYFS separate out the four strands of speaking, listening, reading and writing identified in the Rose Review (2006) into two areas: Communication and language (prime area) and Literacy (specific area). The Tickell Report (2011) explains this:

> …the development of communication and language skills happens during an optimum window of brain development and is experience expectant (therefore…prime)…whereas the acquisition of literacy skills is experience dependent since it can occur at any point in childhood or adulthood. (p.98)

As communication, language and literacy is so inextricably linked I have used ELGs from both these areas in the detailed differentiated activities.

Further reading

Hall, John (February 2005) **Neuroscience and Education – A review of the contribution of brain science to teaching and learning** *Research Report No.121* Scottish Council for Research in Education

Rose, Jim (March 2006) **Independent review of the teaching of early reading** *Final report* Department for Education and Skills

Tickell, Clare (March 2011) **The Early Years: Foundations for life, health and learning** – An Independent Report on the Early Years Foundation Stage to Her Majesty's Government

Department for Education (March 2012) **Statutory Framework for the Early Years Foundation Stage** – Setting the standards for learning, development and care for children from birth to five

Effective learning, observation and assessment

Characteristics of Effective Learning

There are a number of learning characteristics which are evident in all seven areas of learning and development (p.7, 2012). These are not sequential, and it is not possible to identify particular ages or stages when they may be achieved. Learning characteristics include:

- **Playing and exploring** – engagement

- **Active learning** – motivation

- **Creating and thinking critically** – thinking

These learning characteristics should not be considered as an outcome which is summative, or marked in a 'tick list' manner. They represent processes, and may be observed during formative assessment.

Observation

It is crucial to observe children during their participation in these activities in order to assess whether they are working at an appropriate level and to work out their next steps in learning. The differentiation planned in the activity provides suitable challenge for all children.

Children can behave very differently during group, guided, independent and one-to-one opportunities. Some may be very quiet, and appear withdrawn or insecure during a group activity. However, given the opportunity to work with a close friend independently or at a self-chosen activity, a far more confident child may become apparent. Regular observation should therefore be a central part of good early years practice, ensuring that children are observed during different types of activity (guided, shared, self-chosen or independent), in differently sized groups with a range of children and at different times of day.

Sometimes it is useful to have a focus for observation such as an area of development or to discover the style of a child's learning, but at other times it is just as useful to observe the child for a period of time simply to discover what they are all about. If it appears that the child is making good progress, and is able to achieve what is required in an activity it is important to be aware of their next steps in learning. By always providing an opportunity for children to extend their learning they will continue to be interested and motivated, enjoying learning and finding out about new ideas. All of these are valuable personal characteristics which will be necessary throughout the whole of a child's life.

Assessment

The new EYFS will expect practicioners to make judgements as to whether a child is meeting, exceeding or emerging in relation to the Early Learning Goals (ELGs). In addition to their judgements, practicioners will need to make an assessment against the 3 characterisitcs of effective learning (see Observation record sheet page 57). As previously discussed, a child's learning characteristics are not suitable for summative assessment in a 'can they/can't they' manner. Rather, they should be thought of as part of a child's learning journey. It is for this reason that I am not recommending the use of a 'tick list' to record achievement of each learning characteristic. However, a simple observation record could include the characteristics observed during the observation and the context. This would build into a collection of evidence showing each child's strengths and areas for development. An example of an individual observation record of learning characteristics is provided on page 57.

The ELGs in both the prime and specific areas of learning are set at the expected level for a child nearing the end of FS2. Some children may be working towards achieving these goals and some may be exceeding them – it is the nature of any cohort of children. Indeed, there is likely to be discrepancy at times in a child's attainment towards the ELGs between areas of learning – a child rarely makes equal and comparative progress in all areas across a period of a year or more. It is not necessary to record in a numerical manner how a child achieves, but by highlighting the statement which most closely matches the attainment of the child, it is possible to identify their level of understanding and plan the next steps in progressing towards and exceeding the ELGs.

Using the group record sheets

The group record sheets on pages 58-61 can be used to show how a group of children are achieving at any one time – as a snapshot. It does not show progress over time or individual children's next steps but may be useful as a tool to show a co-ordinator or setting leader the strengths and areas for development of a cohort. It is not possible to fit all specific areas of learning onto one sheet so you may need to photocopy some back to back. There are a variety of record sheets here for both specific and prime areas of development. The group record sheet on page 58 for Communication and Language (prime) and Literacy (specific) also gives the opportunity to record achievement in all three areas on the same sheet, as some activities use ELGs from all of these areas. You may choose to use a traffic light system to record where children are in relation to each area of learning.

Rain or shine

Sing a rainbow

The children will be learning to sing 'I can sing a rainbow', signing the colour words using simple sign language such as Makaton or British Sign Language (BSL). Some children could go on to make a simple picture sequence from photographs or picture diagrams, adding labels and captions.

Resources

★ Pictures or diagrams of children signing the song 'I can sing a rainbow' (available online from Makaton and BSL, search on YouTube)

★ Coloured pieces of card in the colours of the rainbow

★ Photographs and pictures of rainbows

★ Film clip of someone signing (these are available for children's programmes)

★ Musical accompaniment/piano score for 'I can sing a rainbow' (optional)

★ Digital camera

★ Facilities for printing the photographs

★ Animal pictures and diagrams of the animal signs

Storybooks

★ 'I Can Sing a Rainbow' song (audio)

★ *A Million Chameleons* by James Young

★ *Red Rockets and Rainbow Jelly* by Sue Heap and Nick Sharratt

Observation and assessment

Communication and Language	Expected statements (ELGs)
Listening and attention	Children listen attentively in a range of situations. They give their attention to what others say and respond appropriately, while engaged in another activity.

Literacy	Expected statements (ELGs)
Writing	Children use their phonic knowledge to write words in ways which match their spoken sounds. They also write some irregular common words. They write simple sentences which can be read by themselves and others. Some words are spelt correctly and others are phonetically plausible.

Key vocabulary

• rainbow	• blue	• sing
• red	• purple	• sign
• orange	• indigo	• deaf
• yellow	• pink	• left
• green	• purple	• right

What to do

Talk to the children about their senses, explaining that some people do not have all their senses and can be visually or hearing impaired. Watch a film clip of a familiar children's programme without the sound on: can the children imagine what it would be like if they could not hear? How would they understand what other people were saying? Explain that there is a recognised way of making signs and symbols which hearing impaired people use to communicate. Watch a clip of someone signing to a children's programme, firstly watch with the sound off and draw the children's attention to the actions used: can they guess what any of it is about? Watch the clip again with sound: how accurate were they?

Tell the children that they are going to learn to sing a song using actions to sign the words. Show the children the pictures of rainbows, explain that they are made of seven colours, and that some of the signs the children will learn will be colour words. Use the key vocabulary where relevant, but ensure that you have explained to the children that the colour words in the song are slightly different to those in a real rainbow. Show them the coloured pieces of card and name the colours clearly for them.

Demonstrate singing the song, then using the action cards or diagrams of the signs slowly teach the children the song and the signs. Keep it simple and demonstrate many times. Encourage all children to participate where possible. If there are some children who are extremely reluctant to sing in a large group then they could hold up the relevant colour card, picture or diagram where relevant.

If this is to be a guided activity…

…then the children can work together with an adult to learn the song and perform the appropriate action. It can be performed to other children in the setting as a large group. If the children are finding it difficult to remember all the signs then divide the group into colour 'teams' and teach them only one or two signs that they perform when it is their turn.

If this is to be an independent activity…

…then show the children where the collection of signs and diagrams will be and allow them to sort them independently – can they recognise the sign and match it to a colour card? Allow them to photograph each other making the different signs. When they have the prints of these photographs ask them to peg the photographs in order on a washing line so that they can sing the song accurately. Provide pencils and paper so that they can make labels for the different colour names or words in the song, for example eyes, ears, sing, rainbow. Attach these to the appropriate photographs.

To support or extend

To support, take a photograph of a child performing each colour word sign. Enlarge these and play a simple matching game. Place all the photographs face down and ask a child to choose one to hold up. As a small group all perform the sign on the photograph card whilst saying the colour word – can they connect the word and the action? Extend this further by holding up coloured objects and asking the children to make the appropriate sign, or by questioning the children to demonstrate their understanding; 'Who has (blue) socks on? Stand up if you are wearing something (red)'. Do not say the colour word, make the sign instead.

To extend the more able children, encourage them to learn more signs for other nouns, for example animals. Have a collection of animal pictures and diagrams showing the appropriate action. Allow the children to use the cards to match and copy the signs. Play games to reinforce these, such as pulling a small farm animal from a feely bag and asking the children to make the matching sign. Try to use these signs when singing familiar songs, such as 'Baa Baa Black Sheep', 'This Little Piggy' or 'Three Blind Mice'.

Ideas for interactive display

Put the photographs of the children making each sign for 'I can sing a rainbow' on a washing line at child height. Provide extra colour cards, word labels and pegs for the children to make their own visual representation of the song. Include blank cards to encourage children to write or draw their own labels and diagrams.

At a simpler level, provide 'easily pegged' coloured clothing such as socks, for the children to arrange the washing in the colour sequence of the rainbow, or provide differently coloured pegs so that the children can simply match the colour of the pegs to the washing on the line.

Parents and carers as partners

At home, learn the signs for 'please', 'thank you', 'hello' and 'goodbye'. Use these together as part of your daily routine. Search on the internet on YouTube and elsewhere for signed programmes and look for simple signs you may understand such as greetings. Can you learn any more simple signs together, such as 'mummy', 'daddy', 'drink' or 'bed'?

Rain or shine

Rainbow arches and bridges

The children will be looking at curves and arches. Using vocabulary linked to mathematical shape and space, they will build arches and bridges with a range of construction materials.

Observation and assessment

Mathematics	Expected statements (ELGs)
Numbers	Children count reliably with numbers from 1 to 20, place them in order and say which number is one more or one less than a given number. They solve problems, including doubling, halving and sharing.
Shape, space and measures	Children use everyday language to talk about size, weight, capacity, position, distance, time and money to compare quantities and objects and to solve problems. They recognise, create and describe patterns. They explore characteristics of everyday objects and shapes and use mathematical language to describe them.

Key vocabulary

- arch
- arched
- curve
- curved
- straight

- round
- 2D
- 3D
- solid
- tall

- wide
- high
- low
- over
- under

Resources

★ Construction and joining toys: Marble run; Lego; train track; car track; Sticklebricks; connecting straws; multilink

★ Small toy animals

★ 2D shapes

★ 3D shapes

★ Feely bag

★ Pictures and photographs of bridges, arches and curved shapes in buildings

★ Digital camera

Storybooks

★ *The Three Billy Goats Gruff* (Traditional Tale)

★ *On the See Saw Bridge* by Koshiro Hata Yuichi Kimura

What to do

Make a simple bridge from construction toys and use it to help tell the children the story of *The Three Billy Goats Gruff*. Use animal toys during the story telling to illustrate the position of the characters, particularly the troll under the bridge and the goats trotting over it. Use the relevant vocabulary, encouraging the children to join in with the repetitive refrains.

Explain to the children that they are going to make bridges from different construction toys, and investigate curves and arches. Show them different pieces of construction, for example a curved piece of car road track, a wooden train bridge, a flat Lego base board. Ask the children to help you sort the items into one of two groups: straight or curved. Introduce the 2D shapes, holding them up and asking the children to say 'straight' or 'curved'. Put the shapes into a feely bag, pulling out a little at each time. Encourage the children to say whether the shape is straight or curved, moving on to name the 2D shapes in anticipation of withdrawing from the bag, e.g. 'It has a straight side…and a curve… it's a semi-circle!' Extend to 3D shapes if appropriate.

If this is to be a guided activity…

…then the children can work together with an adult to make bridges from different construction toys. Give each child a toy animal and ask them to build a bridge wide/long enough to support the animal's weight. Look at the bridges you have built together and talk about their similarities and differences. Extend the activity by giving the children a 'troll' character to put under their bridge – help them to alter their original design to make their bridge tall/wide/long enough to hide the troll character.

If this is to be an independent activity…

…then show the children where the box of resources will be, and explain that they can try this activity sometime this week. Put out a range of toy animals of different sizes along with a selection of different construction materials. Ask them to model the story of *The Three Billy Goats Gruff*, placing the toy animals on their built bridges to test their relative sizes and capabilities. Provide a digital camera for the children to photograph their constructions.

To support or extend

To support, play with construction toys and wooden shapes to make simple curves, bridges and arches. Begin by sorting a collection of wooden shapes or railway track – can they sort it into curved (or arched) and straight? Encourage the children to play with toys such as Marble run and train tracks, modelling and using the key vocabulary whilst playing. Can they build a track without any curves? Does it join up? Can they build a bridge from Lego big enough for a toy car to pass underneath? How can they change the bridge they have built so that a large toy fire engine will pass underneath?

To extend the more able children, encourage them to build bridges using a limited number of pieces of construction. Multilink cubes work well for this. Ask them to build a bridge using only 12 cubes. Look together at the different examples they each made of the bridges – how are they different? Use the mathematical vocabulary of comparative size – taller, shorter, wider, narrower etc. To extend further ask the children to record their multilink bridge by drawing it onto 2 cm squared paper – one cube equals one square on the paper. This is a difficult skill, and you may wish to simplify it by asking them to simply draw around their bridge onto a piece of plain paper, or to photograph it.

Ideas for interactive display

Provide an area for the children to display their models of arches, curves or bridges. Ask questions: 'Who can make a bridge like Evie's?', 'Can anyone make a tunnel from Lego?' Any spectacularly large creations could be photographed and the photograph displayed.

On a simpler level lay out two sorting hoops or sheets of paper labelled 'straight' or 'curved'. Encourage the children to put objects into the relevant group – either random objects from the environment or preselected objects in a basket on the display table.

Put up pictures of arches, curves, bridges and tunnels with clear labels. If possible, include some photographs taken in the local environment that the children recognise. Allow children to put up their own photographs of curved features they have seen.

Parents and carers as partners

At home or when out and about look for curves and arches together. Are there any in the buildings around your home? Do you walk past any on the way to the shops? Do you cross over any bridges or walk through any tunnels on your regular journeys? If you find any examples of arches, curves, bridges or tunnels try to take a photograph which your child can take in to show the other children. (Explain to the parents and carers that if they do not have the facility to print out the photograph it could be viewed at school electronically.

Rain or shine

Making rainbows

The children will be making a rainbow outside on a sunny day by spraying a hosepipe and looking how the sunlight shines through the rain. Following this, they will have the chance to explore prisms and differently coloured cellophane.

Resources

★ An outside space on a sunny day

★ Hose pipe connected to mains water supply

★ Large sheet of white paper

★ Large sheet of black paper

★ Digital camera

★ Selection of prisms and magnifying glasses

★ Torches

★ Coloured cellophane, filters or glasses with coloured lenses

Storybooks

★ *The Rainbow Mystery (Science Solves It)* by Jennifer A. Dussling

★ *What makes a rainbow?* by Betty Ann Schwartz

★ *All the Colours of the Rainbow (Rookie Read About Science)* by Allan Fowler

Observation and assessment

Understanding the world	Expected statements (ELGs)
The world	Children know about similarities and differences in relation to places, objects, materials and living things. They make observations of animals and plants and explain why some things occur, and talk about changes.
Technology	Children recognise that a range of technology is used in places such as homes and schools. They select and use technology for particular purposes.

Key vocabulary

• rain	• water	• orange
• sun	• drops	• yellow
• shine	• hose	• green
• light	• colours	• blue
• shower	• rainbow	• indigo
• spray	• red	• violet

What to do

If you are unsure of how this activity actually occurs it is recommended that you practise it first without the children!

Explain to the children they are going to go outside and try to make a rainbow! Talk with them about the two ingredients necessary for a rainbow in the sky: sunshine (light) and rain (water droplets). Explain that if the light shines through the rain it creates different colours in an arc and this is what a rainbow is. Show the children the hose and water spray and explain that this will represent the water droplets in the atmosphere. Introduce the key vocabulary, recalling the seven colours in a rainbow. Demonstrate spraying the hose, and ask the children to look into the spray to see if they can see any rainbow colours. To highlight the rainbow, hold the sheet of white paper behind the spray to make it easier to distinguish the colours. Equip one of the group (or another adult) with the digital camera in order for them to record an image of the rainbow as it is created. Encourage the children to say the colours they can see. Can they see indigo and violet? Which colour is most prominent, red or violet? Show them how it is more difficult to see the colours in the rainbow when the black paper is placed behind the rainbow. Why do they think this is? Let them each take a turn at holding the hose and 'making a rainbow' themselves.

If this is to be a guided activity…

…then the children can work together with an adult to investigate the way light shines through the different prisms and coloured Cellophanes. Give the children a torch to shine through the objects. Listen carefully to their verbal responses to assess their understanding. Try to extend this with careful questioning, encouraging them to investigate what happens for example when they shine the torch at the end of the prism, 'Now try shining it at the side of the prism. What happens when you hold the prism up to the sunlight at the window and turn it around? Can you make a rainbow appear?'

If this is to be an independent activity…

…then show the children where the basket of resources is and explain that they can try this activity sometime this week. Let them play with the prisms, using the digital camera to photograph any rainbows they create independently. Let them use the pieces of coloured Cellophane to look at the world around them with a coloured tint. Encourage the children to explore how different coloured Cellophane affects differently coloured objects. Following the independent activity ask the children to share their findings and opinions with you – which was their favourite colour? How did the different colours make them feel? What happened when two differently coloured pieces of Cellophane were put together and looked through at the same time?

To support, make a coloured mini-telescope from a short cardboard tube with a piece of coloured Cellophane taped over the end. Encourage the child to look through the tube at differently coloured objects and say what they can see. Can they still identify the colours of objects? Show them some objects of similar shape but different colours, e.g. crayons or pieces of plastic construction. Name the colours of the items and then try the activity again whilst looking through the coloured filter of the mini-telescope. Discuss with the children how the activity was made more difficult. Explore differently-coloured filters or glasses.

To extend the more able children, encourage them to explore the prisms, using a light source to create the rainbow. Can they identify what is the best way to make the rainbow? What is the best position for the light source, and where is the rainbow created? Is it always in the same place? Is it possible to change the size of the rainbow or the density of the colours? Is it possible to turn the rainbow upside down? How could we do this? Observe closely, noting their responses for assessment of their understanding not only of the knowledge but of the skills of scientific enquiry.

Ideas for interactive display

Provide an area with torches, prisms, coloured Cellophane pieces and glasses with coloured lenses for the children to explore and investigate. Include the mini-telescope colour filters. Let other children play with them and talk about what they can see.

Put up pictures of rainbows and different light sources, labelled with colour words and simple vocabulary such as *sun, bulb, candle*.

Parents and carers as partners

At home, collect together coloured translucent plastics and cellophane such as sweet and biscuit wrappers, or food and drink containers. With the supervision of an adult it may be possible to collect some coloured glass items. Put them on a windowsill so that the light shines through – can you help your child to group similar items together, or place the items in the order of the colours of the rainbow? (Red, orange, yellow, green, blue, indigo, violet.)

Play in the bath, sink or outdoors with bubble bath and bubble mixture. Can you see the rainbows in the bubbles?

Rain or shine

Rainbow display

The children will be holding a 'rainbow week', wearing a different colour each day. They will be using craft and collage materials in the colour of the day and creating semi-circle weavings using differently coloured strips of material and papers.

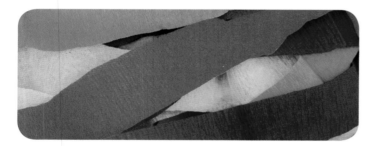

Resources

Separate resources into colours of the rainbow:

★ Collage materials cut into narrow strips no longer than around 30cm (provide different textures, finishes, colours and materials)

★ Drapes/fabric pieces/mats and rugs

★ Paints and paper of different sizes

★ Crayons, pencils and felt-tips

★ Construction toys/bricks

★ Paper plates cut into halves

★ White or black wool or string

★ Pinking shears

★ Pictures showing rainbows

Storybooks and film clips

★ *Elmer and the Rainbow* by David McKee

★ *The Rainbow Fish* by Marcus Pfister

★ *I Eat a Rainbow (My World)* by Bobbie Kalman

Observation and assessment

Expressive arts and design	Expected statements (ELGs)
Exploring and using media and materials	They safely use and explore a variety of materials, tools and techniques, experimenting with colour, design, texture, form and function.
Being imaginative	Children use what they have learnt about media and materials in original ways, thinking about uses and purposes. They represent their own ideas, thoughts and feelings through design and technology, art, music, dance, role-play and stories.

Key vocabulary

- red
- orange
- yellow
- green
- blue
- indigo
- violet
- rainbow
- semi-circle
- weave
- over
- under
- through

What to do

Explain to the children that they are going to create their own rainbow over the week, wearing, playing with and eating (as far as possible) a different colour each day. Discuss with the children the seven colours of the rainbow and point out that there are only five days in the week Monday to Friday. To use seven colours in five days you could choose: Monday: red; Tuesday: orange and yellow; Wednesday: green; Thursday: blue; Friday: pink and purple. Encourage the children to wear something of the daily colour where possible each day, sending home or displaying a notice for parents and carers asking for their support where possible.

On Monday, show the children the activities around the room for the first day, for example red construction toys, red dye in the water tray, red play dough on the malleable table, red sorting animals in the sand with red buckets, red juice and red fruit for snack time, red paper, pens and pencils in the writing area and red collage, paint and paper in the art area.

Show the children the half paper plate and demonstrate how they can cut around the edge of the plate with the pinking shears creating a spiked edge all around the semi-circle. It does not matter at all if this is uneven and irregular as long as there are 'teeth' cut into the edge of the plate. Cut a long length of black or white wool or string and tape one end to the back of the half-plate. Show the children how to wind the wool around the plate as evenly as possible, taping down the end when the wool runs out.

Use this home prepared 'loom' for the children to weave, thread and wrap different strips of collage material over and under, around and through the string. Encourage them to choose their strips independently taking into account colour, texture and finish of the material.

If this is to be a guided activity…

…then the children can work together with an adult to create a rainbow weaving on their paper plate loom. Have pictures of rainbows on the table and talk with the children about which colour they will use first – red or violet? Will it go on the inside or outside of the arc? Help them to select colours they need, justifying their choices.

If this is to be an independent activity…

…then show the children where the box of resources will be, and explain that they can try this activity sometime this week. Provide plenty of collage strips and pictures of rainbows to be used as a stimulus. Have some looms already created so that they can see how to do it, but provide resources for children who wish to make their own.

To support or extend

To support, provide the children with a pre-prepared paper plate 'loom'. Mark onto the plate the seven different coloured sections of the rainbow or simplify it to three or four. Help the children to colour each section with a wax crayon to create a coloured 'rainbow' before showing them the range of collage strips to select from. Let them try to match their coloured plate with a coloured strip, encouraging them to weave in and out, over and under until the wax crayoned coloured section is covered. It may be easier to pass the strip over and under two or three strings, or just to twist and thread randomly until the string is covered.

To extend the more able children, encourage them to work independently to create a weaving of only two or three complementary colours, for example 'warm' (reds, oranges, pinks), 'cool' (blues, purples) or 'natural' (greens, browns). Provide colour shade charts from DIY stores to look at the subtle graduations in shades of a single colour, or to observe how some colours are grouped together into warm and cool. Provide a basket of coloured strips, and encourage the children to justify their choices.

Ideas for interactive display

Provide an area for the children to display their paper plate weavings. Let them try to arrange the weavings next to those of similar colours, e.g. 'mostly red' or 'dark colours'. Ask them to explain their choices.

Put out the role-play fruit, vegetables and other food with a stack of paper plates. Challenge the children to try to design a meal consisting of differently coloured food, or conversely a plate of food all the same colour!

Encourage healthy eating by displaying a poster of a balanced meal, showing the different food groups, or pictures of unusual fruit and vegetables.

Parents and carers as partners

At home, try to encourage healthy eating by offering food of different colours at each mealtime. Make it a game: can the children eat five differently coloured fruit and vegetables each day? Put differently coloured food into a packed lunchbox and play games such as, 'Can you eat something…red?' or 'Please pass me something to eat that is orange!' Cut up old supermarket magazines showing differently coloured food and glue the pictures onto paper plates to make 'menus' – can they find five differently coloured vegetables? Remember to chat with your child when you see fruit and vegetables for sale, to encourage them to try something new.

Select the appropriately coloured T-shirts or socks to wear each day on rainbow coloured week.

Hop, skip and jump

Peter Rabbit's new friend

The children will be reading some of Beatrix Potter's Peter Rabbit stories, looking at the characters and making up a new animal character of their own. They will become aware of some animals that are native to the UK and of their preferred habitats.

Resources

* ★ Beatrix Potter stories and illustrations (search for sites dedicated to Beatrix Potter and Peter Rabbit on the internet)

* ★ Toy animals (limit these to those found in the UK)

* ★ Large pieces of paper

* ★ Pictures or photos of animals from the UK

* ★ Sticky notes

* ★ Junk modelling and construction materials

* ★ Natural and collage materials

Storybooks

* ★ *Peter Rabbit* by Beatrix Potter and other Beatrix Potter stories

* ★ *Percy the Park Keeper* books by Nick Butterworth

* ★ *The Wind in the Willows* stories by Kenneth Williams

* ★ *Hopper Hunts for Spring* by Marcus Pfister

Key vocabulary

* • book
* • author
* • illustrator
* • character
* • assorted animal names

Observation and assessment

Communication and Language	Expected statements (ELGs)
Reading	Children read and understand simple sentences. They use phonic knowledge to decode regular words and read them aloud accurately. They demonstrate understanding when talking with others about what they have read.

Literacy	Expected statements (ELGs)
Speaking	They develop their own narratives and explanations by connecting ideas or events.

What to do

Show the children some of the Beatrix Potter resources. Read some of the stories, talking about the animals in the books. Discuss where the animals are from and where they live – why do you think Beatrix Potter chose these animals to write about? Why not lions, kangaroos or polar bears?

Use the key vocabulary where relevant.

Demonstrate making a character profile on a large piece of paper. Put (or sketch) a picture of Peter Rabbit in the centre. Write around the edge words to describe him, beginning with his physical attributes (furry, brown, blue clothes) and moving onto his personal characteristics (brave, adventurous, hungry!). Encourage all children to contribute where possible. Tell the children that they are going to choose another animal native to the UK and work in a small group to draw it and think of some simple adjectives to describe it, and put these onto sticky notes around the picture. The children can attempt to write or the adult can act as scribe, depending upon the age and ability of the children.

If this is to be a guided activity…

…then the children can work together with an adult to create an animal character profile on a large piece of paper. You could let the children as a class decide which animals they were going to describe, and then let the children join the group doing the animal they were most interested in. 'Expert groups' are then created, and as part of a plenary or feedback time each small group could stand with their character drawing and talk to the rest of the group about their work, justifying and giving reasons for their choices.

If this is to be an independent activity…

…then show the children where the pieces of paper and pictures are and explain that they can choose an animal of their own to describe. Tell them to sketch or glue a picture of their chosen native animal into the centre of their paper, and then attempt to write words around the picture describing their characteristics. Remind them that some can be simple adjectives, but that the higher attaining children may choose to give their animal a personality and select appropriate vocabulary, for example naughty, sneaky, cunning, crafty fox. Discuss their choices.

To support or extend

To support, work with a pair of children to build a character profile of an animal they already know well, for example an animal character from a reading scheme or a favourite book. Encourage the children to draw and colour appropriately the character in the centre of the large piece of paper, and with the adult working as scribe ask the children to say words which describe the character. To help the children when they are trying to think of an adjective have a soft toy or model of the animal so that they can actually hold it.

To extend the more able children, encourage them to create a small world where animal characters may live. Consider carefully the environments of different creatures and try to develop a drawing of a small world, for example a pond, a woodland or a park. Look at books with similar characters, such as *The Wind in the Willows* or *Percy the Park Keeper* to identify animal habitats. Possibly each child could contribute a character profile, building up a character list as a group. Discuss why it would be more likely that a frog would be friends with a duck than an owl – they share a similar habitat! To extend even further, provide resources to enable the children to physically construct their imaginary habitat, using junk modelling, construction, small world animals and natural collage materials. This could be left in a tuff spot all week for other children to add to.

Ideas for interactive display

- Put the collection of books and illustrations by Beatrix Potter, Kenneth Williams and Nick Butterworth on a low table for the children to look at. Put an accompanying set of small animals from around the world in a basket – can the children sort the animals into those native to the UK and those from other countries? Or on a simpler level, can they find and identify those from the stories?

- Put up the large character profile sheets for the children to look at the labels and captions chosen. Leave a pen and some sticky notes on the display – can they add any more words or labels of their own? Encourage them to write independently, making phonetically plausible attempts at unknown words.

Parents and carers as partners

At home, try to visit the library to look for books about animals from the UK. Talk together about wildlife in the local environment, helping your child to recognise that some animals have particular habitats (desert, jungle, arctic) and that the only way they can survive in the UK is in captivity. Make a picture together of all the animals that might live in your area.

Hop, skip and jump

Jumping numbers

The children will be using number lines to practise counting forwards and backwards. They will be jumping forwards and backwards whilst saying number names in order, adding and subtracting. If appropriate this activity can be extended to counting in multiples of two, five and ten; teaching multiplication as repeated addition.

Resources

★ Large number line either chalked on the ground, or individual carpet tiles painted with numerals

★ Large numeral cards

★ Large operation symbols including + - =

Storybooks

★ *Ten Little Speckled Frogs* song (audio)

★ *Jump, Frog, Jump!* by Robert Kalan

★ *Snow Rabbit, Spring Rabbit: A Book of Changing Seasons* by Il Sung Na

Observation and assessment

Mathematics	Expected statements (ELGs)
Numbers	Children count reliably with numbers from 1 to 20, place them in order and say which number is one more or one less than a given number. Using quantities and objects, they add and subtract two single-digit numbers and count on or back to find the answer. They solve problems, including doubling, halving and sharing.
Shape, space and measures	Children use everyday language to talk about size, weight, capacity, position, distance, time and money to compare quantities and objects and to solve problems. They recognise, create and describe patterns.

Key vocabulary

- more
- less
- forwards
- backwards
- add
- subtract
- groups
- multiples
- number names
- numeral
- digit
- hop
- jump

What to do

Explain to the children that they are going to jump along like frogs or rabbits, counting in order forwards and backwards. As a warm up sing 'Ten Little Speckled Frogs'. Select ten children to stand in a line, taking turns to hop off the imaginary log into the water. Give each of the ten children a number card 1–10 to hold, firstly asking them to put themselves into order in a line. Count forwards and backwards up and down the line before singing the song. Introduce the symbols cards, ensuring that all of the children recognise the mathematical symbols + and =. Make a number sentence with a total under five, e.g. $2 + 3 = 5$. Use the number and symbol cards to order the sentence, using children to count. For example, ask two children to stand together, and ask another three children to stand together in a different group. Put the '+' sign between them, and explain that this means 'altogether'. Demonstrate physically moving the children into one large group and counting them. Show the '=' card, and put into the number sentence. Repeat as many times as necessary until the children understand the sequence of a number sentence. Encourage the correct use of key vocabulary.

Explain that another way to add three to two is to 'count on' along a number line. Show the children the large number line on the floor, and choose a child to hop along it whilst everyone counts up. Note that as the child moves forward the numbers get bigger and vice versa. Use the number and symbol cards to make the same number sentence as before. Demonstrate by asking a child to stand on number 2, and jump on three times. (Ensure that the children count the actual jump and not the number they are standing on to begin with – this is a common mistake). Have they landed on 5? So two and three makes five! Repeat as necessary until children have grasped the concept. Link the physical jumping on along the number line to pointing at a smaller fixed number line, and write the matching number sentence each time.

If appropriate this activity can be used at a later date to jump in multiples, demonstrating multiplication as repeated addition.

If this is to be a guided activity…

…then the children can work together with an adult to make their own number sentences and additions. Use the large number line on the floor to find the answer to simple sums requiring 'add 1'. Have the sums written on a flipchart with a box for the answer. Support the children to take turns to jump along the number line until they have the answer, then write the answer in the correct place in the number sentence. Continue, with the children making up their own sums and challenging their friends to find the answer using the number line.

If this is to be an independent activity…

…then show the children where the numbered carpet tiles or large numbered pieces of paper are and tell them that they are to use this equipment to answer some simple additions and subtractions. Have some sums ready prepared on a flipchart, or to differentiate the activity have some ready prepared sheets colour coded into different levels of difficulty. Encourage the children to work with a friend or two to find the answers – laying out the numbered tiles in sequence, finding the beginning number, jumping along and recording the answer.

To support or extend

To support, focus upon adding one each time. Work in pairs or a very small group, where one child is the jumping frog and the others the counter. Let the jumping frog choose a number to stand on, and ask the other children to predict which number they will land on each time when one is added. Extend firstly to adding two, then three. If the children are able, move on to jumping backwards, counting backwards from five and ten, and subtracting one.

To extend this activity use simple bead threading, coloured bricks or coloured pegs and boards to make and show number bonds. Choose a number less than ten, e.g. six, and give the children two piles of differently coloured pegs/beads/bricks. Ask them to make some towers/threaded beads/lines of pegs which total six, but use two differently coloured sets. For example, one red plus five blue; two red plus four blue; three red plus three blue. Challenge the children to find as many different ways as they can to make different numbers up to ten or 12. Let them record pictorially, using their recordings as examples of emergent mathematics, or keep their patterns for display and discussion.

Ideas for interactive display

- Put a set of number tiles or hoops with number cards out and challenge the children to put them in order. Let them practise jumping forwards and backwards, counting in order as they go. Extend the activity by beginning the number cards at 11, or by only putting out odd numbers or multiples of two or ten.

- Provide sets of counters/pegs/beads to thread and challenge the children to use them to make number patterns with the same total number of beads/pegs, but using different colours.

- Create an outdoor display by hanging a number washing line or by chalking the beginning of a number line. Provide extra chalk for the children to create number lines of their own.

Parents and carers as partners

At home, use chalk to draw number lines or hopscotch on the ground. Play together, saying the numbers when you are hopping and jumping along. Count items you see when out and about – paving slabs, railings, chairs, windows. Help your child to notice patterns – one red railing then two blue railings; two little steps then two big steps; one table with a stool at each corner. Talk about how many, more and less, one more, forwards and backwards. Noticing and commenting upon patterns and numbers is a good foundation for early mathematical ability.

Hop, skip and jump

Paper plate lifecycles

The children will be learning about the lifecycle of a frog, and making a representation of this on a paper plate by drawing and collage.

Observation and assessment

Understanding the world	Expected statements (ELGs)
The world	Children know about similarities and differences in relation to places, objects, materials and living things. They make observations of animals and plants and explain why some things occur, and talk about changes.

Key vocabulary

- frog
- frogspawn
- tadpole
- egg
- lifecycle
- old
- young

Resources

★ White cardboard paper plates (unwaxed is easier to draw on)

★ Paper fasteners/split pins

★ Bubble wrap

★ Coloured card

★ Pencil/wax crayons

★ Pictures and photographs of frogs, tadpoles and frogspawn

Storybooks

★ *The Trouble with Tadpoles: A First Look at the Life Cycle of a Frog* by Sam Godwin and Simone Abel

★ *From Tadpole to Frog (Lifecycles)* Gerald Legg and Carolyn Scrace

To support, have most of the materials pre-prepared. Provide photocopied picture outlines of tadpoles and frogs for the children to simply colour in so that they do not have to draw them. Simplify the lifecycle to only three stages if necessary: frogspawn, tadpole and frog. Work with only one or two children at a time, modelling the key vocabulary as the lifecycle is constructed.

To extend this activity, encourage the children to represent the lifecycles of other living things, for example egg, chick and hen, or human baby, child and adult. Provide simple non-fiction books of different living things for the children to use for ideas. The method of paper plate, split pin and pointing arrow may remain the same, but they could choose a different subject independently.

What to do

Read *The Trouble with Tadpoles* together. Talk about the lifecycle of a frog; tell the children that frogs lay eggs in ponds, but that the eggs are not in hard shells but in a kind of jelly. Use the appropriate key vocabulary as you explain this lifecycle. Finally explain that the reason it is called a 'cycle' is that it goes round and round as the adult frogs create more frogspawn. Draw parallels with bicycle wheels and the way they turn.

Explain to the children they are going to make a picture to show the different stages in the life of a frog, using a paper plate. Show them a finished lifecycle plate with a coloured card arrow fixed into the centre like the hands on a clock. Around the edge of the plate discuss in turn each of the stages: frogspawn, young tadpole, mature tadpole, young frog, adult frog.

Demonstrate making and affixing the arrow pointer with the split pin. Show the children the bubble wrap – what could it be used to represent? Cut a small piece and glue onto the plate. Show them how and where to draw the remaining tadpole and frog pictures. Finish by drawing arrows between each stage, around the edge of the plate, showing the direction of the cycle.

If this is to be a guided activity…

…then the children can work together with an adult to create their own frog lifecycle plate. Talk with the children at each stage of the activity, modelling the key vocabulary and cutting skills necessary. Encourage the children to try to measure the length of the cardboard pointing arrow and the area of the piece of bubble wrap independently. Don't be tempted to prepare the resources or an opportunity for the children to select, create and use resources independently will be missed.

If this is to be an independent activity…

…then show the children where the resources are laid out and explain that they will try this activity sometime this week. For safety reasons an adult may need to pre-punch a small hole in the paper plate for the split pin to pass through, depending upon the age and capabilities of the children. Provide some simple non-fiction books and photographs of frogs, tadpoles and frogspawn for the children to use for information when drawing.

Ideas for interactive display

Put the collection of books and photographs of different lifecycles on a table for the children to look at. Include a selection of jigsaws or dominoes showing animals old and young (e.g. horses and foals, or dogs and puppies) or different stages in an animal's life.

Encourage the children to bring in photographs of themselves now and as a baby. Talk about changes and growing. Can the children guess who the baby photographs are?

Parents and carers as partners

At home, look at photographs of your child as a baby. Talk together about growing up and the different stages. If it is possible, look at photographs of other family members at different stages in their life, to help your child to understand that everyone was once a baby and that it is inevitable that everyone grows older.

Hop, skip and jump

Wagging tails, floppy ears and jumping legs

The children will be making a moving picture from card, with a wagging lamb's tail, floppy rabbit ears and springing frog's legs.

Observation and assessment

Expressive arts and design	Expected statements (ELGs)
Exploring and using media and materials	They safely use and explore a variety of materials, tools and techniques, experimenting with colour, design, texture, form and function.
Being imaginative	Children use what they have learnt about media and materials in original ways, thinking about uses and purposes. They represent their own ideas, thoughts and feelings through design and technology, art, music, dance, role-play and stories.

Resources

* Coloured card of different sizes and colours (include colour suitable for rabbits, lambs and frogs)

* A4 pieces of card (for background)

* Cotton wool balls

* Pieces of foil

* Green strips of paper

* Scissors

* Paper fasteners/split pins

* Glue

* Digital camera

Storybooks and film clips

* *Marvin Wanted More* by Joseph Theobald

* *In Like a Lion, Out Like a Lamb* by Marion Dane Bauer

* *When will it be Spring* by Catherine Walters

* *What do you do with a tail like this?* by Steve Jenkins and Robin Page

* *Valentine* by Carol Carrick

Key vocabulary

* lamb
* sheep
* kitten
* rabbit
* cut
* fold
* bend
* pierce

What to do

Explain to the children that they are going to make a picture showing some animals common in spring, including rabbits, lambs and frogs. Talk about where you may find these animals (habitats). Sketch on a flipchart a wavy line bisecting the paper left to right, representing a rolling hill: draw a pond shape at the bottom of the paper, draw a small circle near the bottom of the hill to represent a rabbit hole. Ask the children to say where they think you would find a rabbit, a lamb and a frog. Roughly sketch the frog and the lamb onto the paper. The rabbit is to be represented by two ears poking out of the rabbit hole!

Rabbits: cut two rabbit ear shapes from card and bend or curl them around a pencil or your finger. Glue these curled over floppy ears onto the rabbit hole.

Frogs: fold two green strips of paper forwards, backwards, forwards, backwards as though making a fan. These become two boingy frog legs, attached to the sketch of the frog by glue.

Lambs: cut a lamb's tail from card, gluing on cotton wool. Show the children how to push a split pin through the tail and wag it from side to side.

Show the children the A4 piece of card, explaining that they are to make a picture including one, two or all of the animals.

If this is to be a guided activity…

…then the children can work together with an adult to create their pictures. Model each step simply, allowing the children to investigate and explore the materials and skills by themselves. Use the key vocabulary, and encourage the children to become more precise in their discussions, e.g. 'I'm going to fold that piece a bit wider next time/this rabbit ear is shorter than the other and I want them to look the same'.

If this is to be an independent activity…

…then show the children where the box of resources will be, and explain that they can try this activity sometime this week. Simplify the picture by requiring only one moving part or 3D effect such as curled paper. The children could make a card instead, celebrating spring. Provide outlines of animals or stencils of the moving parts for the children to trace or colour and stick onto their picture/card.

To support or extend

To support, begin by using construction which may hinge or pivot, such as Meccano. Let the children play with it and explore its properties and movements. During play begin to draw some parallels with real life movements, for example 'This part moves like a seesaw!', 'Can you make a wagging tail?'. Depending upon the age and ability of the children, they could make a simple picture with one moving part, such as a wagging tail. Prepare resources beforehand so that they need only combine the parts to make a picture.

To extend the more able children, encourage them to work independently to create other moving pictures. Show them how to cut a slit in a card background in order to poke through a slider, made from a straw with a picture stuck on the end. This enables them to add a moving part either horizontally or vertically. They can draw a background scene, for example the night sky, and then add zooming rockets or shooting stars.

Ideas for interactive display

- Put out a selection of construction materials for children to investigate: can they make a simple pivot or lever?

- Display photographs of objects familiar to the children, such as playground equipment, scissors, door handles and clock hands. Can they think of any others? Leave the camera on the display so that if a child discovers another moving part they can fetch the camera to photograph it. Display these along with any photographs the children bring in from home.

Parents and carers as partners

At home, look for pivots and hinges (such as seesaws, swings, scissors, door handles and windows) in the area and buildings around you. A walk to the local play area may provide lots of examples: look at each moving object and talk with your child about how it works, does it remind them of anything else? A swing, for example, moves a little like a horse's tail or a clock pendulum. Don't worry about using the correct scientific terms for things – just talk about what you see around you. If you were to photograph them your child could share the photographs back in the setting with their friends.

Blooming blossoms

How to plant a bulb

The children will be writing simple instructions on how to plant a bulb in a flowerpot, and illustrating appropriately.

Observation and assessment

Literacy	Expected statements (ELGs)
Writing	Children use their phonic knowledge to write words in ways which match their spoken sounds. They also write some irregular common words. They write simple sentences which can be read by themselves and others. Some words are spelt correctly and others are phonetically plausible.

Key vocabulary

- bulb
- plant
- flower

- stem
- root
- shoot

- pot
- water
- light

Resources

- ★ Spring bulbs such as amaryllis, paper white narcissus, hyacinth or crocus bulbs (try to find ones that are ready to be forced, or that have already had a cool period to stimulate growth)

- ★ Plant pots

- ★ Compost or soil

- ★ Small, filled watering can

- ★ Ruler

- ★ Flipchart or whiteboard

- ★ A4 paper

Storybooks

- ★ *Fletcher and the Springtime Blossoms* by Julia Rawlinson

- ★ *From Bud to Blossom/From Blossom to Fruit* by Gail Saunders-Smith

What to do

Discuss with the children where plants come from and how they grow. Look at some simple non-fiction books together. Talk about seeds, stones in fruit and bulbs: how many of the children have encountered these? Have some to show the children. Explain that these must not be eaten but that they are all the beginning of a plant. Select which type of bulb or bulbs you are to grow in your class. It may be simpler to buy a kit for a large bulb such as an amaryllis and plant it together as a class than to give each child an individual bulb of, for example, paper whites narcissus.

Explain to the children that they are going to plant a bulb in a pot, and then wait for it to grow a shoot and flower. Show the children the equipment using the key vocabulary where relevant.

Demonstrate how to plant the bulb, showing filling the pot with compost, placing the bulb the correct way up and watering gently. Explain to the children that they are going to help another class or group of children plant a bulb by writing and drawing some instructions explaining what they did. Ask the children to tell you what they did, and recreate their instructions. For example, if they say, 'Put the bulb in the pot' simply drop the upside down bulb into the empty pot. When the children laugh or say something, ask 'Is that not what you said?' Ask them for more detailed information. After each step, model writing it on the flipchart or whiteboard in a simple caption or sentence. Include an illustration at each step.

If this is to be a guided activity…

…then the children can work together with an adult to create a simple folded book showing the sequence of planting a bulb. Firstly lay out the items needed, and ask the children to draw and label these on the front of the folded piece of paper, as on the cover of a book. Encourage the children to work independently where possible, using their phonic knowledge to write labels underneath their pictures. Inside the book use the next three sides to draw pictures to show the planting stages:

1. Fill the pot with compost and make a hole for the bulb.

2. Place the bulb in the pot and cover with compost.

3. Water the bulb every day.

If this is to be an independent activity…

…then show the children the table with the bulb, compost, pot and watering can. Provide labels for each item. On small whiteboards, encourage the children to draw a picture or pictures to illustrate how to plant the bulb. Encourage the children to work independently where possible, using their phonic knowledge to write labels underneath their pictures. These can be kept and photocopied by an adult as examples of the child's emergent writing.

To support or extend

To support, put differently sized pots in the sand tray, with compost and some beans, seeds and bulbs to plant. The seeds do not have to be viable plants, instead you can provide dried beans, peas, lentils and small onions for the children to play and experiment with. Put out trays with differently sized arrays and compartments: use a range of egg boxes, chocolate box inserts, fruit and vegetable packaging with differently sized dents and different yoghurt pots. Let the children play at 'planting', using differently sized spoons, spades and trowels to fill the differently sized pots. Encourage them to record what they have done by drawing pictures of their choice of container, seed and tool to fill the container with compost. Use simple mathematical vocabulary, encouraging them to question decisions they are making and beginning to predict and discriminate.

To extend this activity encourage the children to write simple instructions on how to do another familiar task, such as washing their hands. Look at some simple non-fiction texts together, identifying the key features such as titles, numbered sentences, bullet points, information boxes and illustrations. Help the children to make information posters showing how to wash hands. These could be laminated and displayed around the setting for other children to refer to.

Ideas for interactive display

Put out a selection of beans, seeds and bulbs for the children to look at, group and sort. Leave some sticky labels for them to label their groups, e.g. small and round; brown; speckled.

Find some plants and vegetables in their natural state and lay them out, for example a carrot with roots and a green top, or a daffodil from roots to flower. Let the children look at and handle them, encouraging them to make some observational drawings of what they can see. Display these drawings on the wall above the table display.

Parents and carers as partners

At home, encourage your child to be interested in how things grow and where food comes from. Look at vegetables such as onions, leeks and carrots, and explain that these all grow roots down into the soil. See if you can see the roots, or where they were. Try growing a bean in a glass or a jam jar; roll up some kitchen towel and drop loosely into the glass so that it is rubbing against the sides. Wedge a bean between the paper towel and the glass, and pour in a little water so that the towel becomes wet. The bean will send out a root and then a shoot, which is visible through the glass. If it is planted in compost it may even produce beans to eat!

Blooming blossoms

Pennies and flowers: how much?

The children will be using 1p and 2p coins to make simple additions on flower petals.

Observation and assessment

Mathematics	Expected statements (ELGs)
Shape, space and measures	Children use everyday language to talk about size, weight, capacity, position, distance, time and money to compare quantities and objects and to solve problems.

Key vocabulary

- coin
- copper
- silver
- gold
- 1p
- 2p
- penny
- pence
- two pence
- flower
- petal

Resources

- ★ Coins of each denomination

- ★ Plenty of 1p coins

- ★ Large laminated outline of a flower, with each petal big enough for a 1p coin

- ★ Variety of smaller flower outlines with different number of petals

- ★ Small whiteboards and pens

- ★ Photocopies of small pennies, individually cut out, or a 1p stamper

- ★ Wax crayons in copper and bronze

Storybooks

- ★ *Buds and Blossoms: A Book About Flowers* by Susan Blackaby

- ★ *The Great Pet Sale* by Mick Inkpen

What to do

Explain to the children that they are going to learn about coins and money. Read *The Great Pet Sale* and talk about the cost of the rat: only 1p! Show the children the different coins. Ask them if they know how much any of the coins are worth, and Blu-tack them to the board in order of value.

Introduce the laminated picture of the flower with, for example, five large petals. Put a 1p coin in each of the petals, and let the children count aloud with you how much money there is altogether. Stress the word 'pence' or 'p' after each number name, and say 'Five p altogether' at the end. Write '5p' in the centre of the flower with a whiteboard marker.

Demonstrate again with another flower with a different number of petals. Explain to the children that the number of pennies is the total amount altogether, and that this is the amount the flower costs. Encourage all the children to show you on their fingers how much each flower will cost before counting together as a group.

If this is to be a guided activity…

…then the children can work together with an adult to create their own number flower. Begin as a group with identical five petal flowers and let the children stamp, stick or draw the pennies into the petals and write the total sum in the centre. Differentiate the number of petals on the flower drawings for the children to work at an appropriate level. Children may wish to work as a group on a large piece of paper, for example wall lining paper, to create a 'garden' with a flower of each value up to 10p, or beyond.

If this is to be an independent activity…

…then explain to the children that a corner of the room is going to become a flower shop, and that their role is to create the flowers worth different amounts. Put out a selection of flower outlines with different number of petals. Ask the children to draw, stick or stamp pennies onto the petals and write the total amount (cost) of the flower in the centre. This activity may be extended by counting in multiples, such as 2ps, 5ps or 10p. As a challenge you may provide the outline of a stem and a flower centre with an amount, but without petals – how can they make this amount?

To support or extend

To support, use 1p coins up to 5p, and have a 5p coin. Explain to the children that each flower petal is worth 1p, and put these on a drawing of a stem and a flower centre. Begin with just the stem drawing, and place the 1p on as a petal. Explain that this is a very old and broken flower with only one petal so it is only worth 1p. Repeat with different amounts of 1p petals, up to 5p. Keep counting and checking the amount. Write the amount in the centre each time. Finally, when there are five penny petals on the flower explain that the flower is complete, and that the 5p coin can go in the centre to show it is complete.

To extend the more able children, encourage them to draw their own flowers worth different amounts. How many petals on a flower worth 6p? If they are able to count in twos substitute the 1p coins for 2p coins. How many petals now on a flower worth 6p? Or 10p? Is there a pattern? Children able to count in fives and tens may use these coins as petals, and count in multiples. Encourage the children to use the whiteboards to record their working and thinking by drawing pictures and mark making. Keep these for later discussion and as an example of early emergent mathematics – whiteboards photocopy really well!

Ideas for interactive display

* Have a washing line and pegs with large copies of coins. Can the children order the coins into value, least to most? Have different items with price labels up to 10p. Let the children put the correct amount of money against each item, playing 'shopping'.

* Put out some whiteboards and pens and some money challenges – can they draw a flower worth 7p? How many petals on a flower worth 10p?

Parents and carers as partners

At home, use coins of small denomination for counting, matching, sorting and ordering. Give your child a handful of 1p, 2p, 5p and 10p coins and help them to sort into piles. Look carefully at the designs and patterns on the coins – are all the 1p coins the same, for instance? Encourage your child to begin to use coins to pay for small items, e.g. a newspaper or a stamp, so that they become used to seeing and using them. For many children nowadays actual coins are a rarity as adults often pay with bank or credit cards!

Blooming blossoms

Growing cress heads

The children will be growing cress in the top of an eggshell. They will decorate the eggshell like a person, and the growing cress will become crazy hair! Extend to growing grass seed to make an environment.

Observation and assessment

Understanding the world	Expected statements (ELGs)
The world	Children know about similarities and differences in relation to places, objects, materials and living things. They talk about the features of their own immediate environment and how environments might vary from one another. They make observations of animals and plants and explain why some things occur, and talk about changes.

Key vocabulary

- cress
- grass
- seed
- water
- wet
- dry
- cotton wool
- paper towel
- eggshell

Resources

- ★ Eggshells, broken in half
- ★ Egg boxes or egg cups
- ★ Cress seed
- ★ Cotton wool
- ★ A punnet of grown cress from the greengrocer
- ★ Large flat trays/foil tins
- ★ Grass seed, mixed bird seed, sunflower seeds and other types of seed
- ★ Paper or kitchen towel to grow grass seed in
- ★ Small world creatures and animals

Storybooks

- ★ *Growing Things (Circle of Life)* by Carolyn Scarce
- ★ *The Pea Blossom* by Amy Lowry Poole
- ★ *How Do Plants Grow? (Young Explorer: World of Plants)* by Louise Spilsbury

What to do

Explain to the children they are going to grow some cress from seed and show them the punnet of grown cress. Take off the plastic punnet and let the children see the material it is grown in, the seeds, roots and cress. Pass it around so that each child can hold it and look closely. Talk about how it feels – wet/dry, heavy/light? Show the children the packet of dry seeds. Discuss what seeds need to grow: water, light and material to grow in.

Introduce the key vocabulary whilst showing the items needed for the investigation. Explain to the children that they are going to grow some cress in an empty eggshell. Demonstrate putting the cotton wool in and sprinkling a few seeds on the top. Water gently, and let the children look at the seeds before they begin to grow.

Over the next few days look regularly at the eggshell, looking for signs of sprouting and growing. Discuss the changes observed. When the cress finally begins to sprout over the top, draw a face onto the shell to give your cress egg head a personality!

If this is to be a guided activity…

…then the children can work together with an adult to create their cress egg head. Model the use of the key vocabulary whilst helping the children to put the cotton wool in the eggshell and use words like sprinkle and pour. Each day, gather the same group of children together to look at the cress seeds – is anything happening to them? Is it happening to each eggshell at the same time? Why do you think some are growing faster/ stronger than others? Encourage children to notice the amount of water, density of seeds sown and amount of light received by each eggshell when making their comments.

If this is to be an independent activity…

…then show the children where the seeds, cotton wool and eggshells are and explain that they can try this activity sometime this week. As modelled in the main activity, the children are to create a cress egg head. They can draw a face on the eggshell with felt tips before the cress begins to grow.

Encourage the children to keep a simple visual diary of the progress of the growing cress – fold a strip of paper forwards and backwards into a simple zig zag book. Write the days of the week at the top of each page and explain to the children that they are to draw what their eggshell cress looks like each day.

To support or extend

To support, work with each child to look at the dry cress seeds and the picture on the packet. Talk about how the seeds look, sound and feel. Explain that they will not grow without water and light, and that they are to plant some in some wet cotton wool inside an eggshell. Support the child whilst planting. If they find it difficult to sprinkle on either the dry seed or a small amount of water provide a shaker, such as a spice container or a homemade lid made from pierced foil. Look each day at the changes and take photographs. These can be used for ordering after the cress has grown.

To extend the more able children, encourage them to plant a small environment in a flattish foil tray. Lay out wet paper kitchen towel, and choose different seeds to sow onto different areas of the tray. Look at some different seeds – cress, grass seed, mixed bird seed and individual seeds such as sunflower or peas and beans. Mark out different areas of the tray with small pebbles or stones, and sow different seeds into different areas. The seeds may grow at different rates but this is not a problem – it is exciting waiting to see what will pop up! When the environment is grown encourage the children to add some small world creatures or people to populate it. The children may wish to repeat this activity when they have seen how each plant grows, so that they can create a 'field', 'wood' or 'lawn'. Add other natural materials such as stones and twigs to create boulders and fences.

Ideas for interactive display

- Put out the different growing plants for the children to look at. Gather together a collection of different house plants in pots for the children to look at and talk about. Make templates of the different leaf shapes – can they identify the plant by the shape of the leaf?

- Provide sequencing cards or jigsaws of a plant growing from seed: can they order it correctly? Include photographs taken of their own cress growing day by day.

Parents and carers as partners

At home, try growing some different plants from seed on the windowsill. Cheap birdseed is a very entertaining 'crop' to grow, as you never quite know what will pop up! Of course, this is not edible – if you want an edible result and can buy a packet of seed, cress is a quick growing edible crop. Lettuce or mixed leaves also grows very successfully in a small pot or trough, as do many herbs.

Blooming blossoms

Japanese blow painting

The children will be making paintings in the style of traditional Japanese paintings of blossom, by blowing paint through a straw and adding pink blossom using their fingertips and cotton buds as a brush.

Resources

★ Watered down paint, in dark brown

★ Small pieces of paper

★ Straws

★ Cotton buds

★ White, pale pink and deep pink paint

★ Examples of traditional Japanese paintings of blossom and flowers (do an image search on the internet)

Storybooks

★ *Japanese Celebrations: Cherry Blossoms, Lanterns and Stars!* by Betty Reynolds

★ *Cherry Blossom Festival colouring and activity book* by Carole Marsh

★ *Underneath the Cherry Blossom Tree: An Old Japanese Tale* retold by Allen Say

Observation and assessment

Expressive arts and design	Expected statements (ELGs)
Exploring and using media and materials	They safely use and explore a variety of materials, tools and techniques, experimenting with colour, design, texture, form and function.
Being imaginative	Children use what they have learnt about media and materials in original ways, thinking about uses and purposes. They represent their own ideas, thoughts and feelings through design and technology, art, music, dance, role-play and stories.

Key vocabulary

- brush
- dab
- twig
- straw
- dot
- stem
- blow
- fingertip
- blossom
- paint
- cotton bud
- flower

What to do

Safety first!
Make sure the children blow carefully down the straws and do not suck up the paint.

Explain to the children that they are going to create a painting in the style of a traditional Japanese painting and show them some examples. Talk about how the brush strokes can create thick or thin stems and twigs, and how they are wider at the beginning and thinner at the end of the twig. Look at the blossom and flowers: are they all the way along each twig or do they cluster? Are they all the same size or are some larger or smaller than others?

Demonstrate putting a blob of watery paint onto the bottom edge of the paper and blowing through the straw to move the paint along in a line. Show the children how this looks like a twig. Blow other 'twigs' onto the picture. Encourage the children to keep looking at their picture as they go, carefully deciding where the next 'twig' should be. Demonstrate how the blossom can be created by finger painting dots onto the twig. Show the children how to choose their different colours for different size dots and different colours. The cotton buds can also be used for a similar effect.

If this is to be a guided activity…

…then the children can work together with an adult to create their own painting in the style of a traditional Japanese cherry blossom picture. Allow the children to select the colour and size of paper they like, and put an actual stem of blossom on the table. Spend some time looking together at what the children can actually see – often children presume what it will look like and need an adult to draw their attention to what is actually there in front of them! Count the buds, the petals – are there the same number of petals on each bloom? Whereabouts are the blooms on the stem? Keep reminding the children to look carefully while they are painting. Keep the medium the same (e.g. paint) but allow the children to change and select their paper.

If this is to be an independent activity…

…then show the children where the activity is set up on the art table and explain to them that they can do some observational artwork this week. Some children may choose to return to the activity more than once. The stem of blossom which they are drawing and observing may start to change in appearance over the week, and it may be a good idea to record on each picture which day it was made. The series of pictures could then be displayed, along with a photograph each day. Blossom quickly loses its freshness when cut and kept inside.

Provide a variety of paper and equipment for the children to experiment with.

To support or extend

To support, let the children create their own 'blossom' by screwing up small pieces of tissue paper and gluing it onto actual twigs collected from outside. Encourage them to look at real blossom (photographs or outdoors) and to choose appropriate colours of tissue paper – is there blue or black blossom in nature? Following this, encourage them to try to blow paint along with a straw and use their fingers to paint blossom. With younger children this is best done with only one or two children at a time, or paint gets everywhere!

To extend the more able children, encourage them to work independently to create other Japanese style paintings. Look at an artist such as Hokusai, and study some of his well-known 'Wave' pictures. Compare them, encouraging the children to talk about which pictures they like or dislike. Can they give a reason? Give each child a small 'viewer' – a piece of card around A6 size with the centre cut out to leave a frame. Show them how to move their frame around a picture, selecting a part they particularly like. Why do they like this part? Have they chosen the same part as anyone else?

Ideas for interactive display

The paintings look very attractive displayed together on a wall, as they are so similar yet all unique. If possible, collect some actual blossom twigs and branches for the display table, and provide differently sized and coloured pieces of paper and different media to draw in, e.g. chalk, pencil, charcoal, felt tip and pastel. Let the children do some observational drawings of the blossom in different media. Discuss as a group – which method is most successful? Why? Does it look better in white, black or pink paper? Why?

Parents and carers as partners

At home, experiment by painting using different tools, not just a brush. Items such as cotton buds, toothbrushes, Lego bricks and the child's own hands and fingers can all be used in paint to press, print, draw and spread different marks and patterns. If your child is a prolific artist and you cannot replace the paper quickly enough try taping a black plastic sack to a table or the floor, squirt on some paint and let them use their hands in the paint, drawing and moving the paint around the plastic. This can then be gathered up and thrown away.

Eggs and chicks

Zig-zag book: from egg to hen

The children will be using concertina folded strips of paper to make a book, showing the different stages in the lifecycle of a chicken, from egg to hen.

Observation and assessment

Communication and Language	Expected statements (ELGs)
Listening and attention	Children listen attentively in a range of situations. They listen to stories, accurately anticipating key events and respond to what they hear with relevant comments, questions or actions. They can give their attention to what others say and respond appropriately, while engaged in another activity.

Literacy	Expected statements (ELGs)
Writing	Children use their phonic knowledge to write words in ways which match their spoken sounds. They also write some irregular common words.

Resources

★ Paper and card of different shapes, sizes and colours

★ Selection of writing and drawing materials

★ Large poster-sized piece of paper

★ Simple non-fiction texts

★ Stapler

★ Hole punch

★ String

★ Treasury tags

Storybooks

★ *From Egg to Chicken (Lifecycles)* by Gerald Legg and Carolyn Scrace

★ *Hatch, Egg, Hatch!* (A touch and feel action flap book) by Shen Ruddie and Frances Cony

★ *The Cow That Laid an Egg* by Andy Cutbill

★ *Eggs and Chicks* (Usbourne Beginners) by Fiona Patchett

Key vocabulary

- egg
- chick
- hen
- lifecycle
- folding
- concertina

What to do

Discuss the stages in the lifecycle of a hen: from egg to chick to hen. Explain that the female hen then lays another egg and it begins again. Look together at some of the simple non-fiction books, and talk about the clear pictures, titles and headings and how these give information. Use the key vocabulary where relevant. Tell the children that they are going to write their own non-fiction book about eggs, chicks and hens, and that other children are going to look at it to find out information. This will give the children a purpose for writing.

Demonstrate folding a strip of paper forwards and backwards on itself to make a concertina style book. These can be pre-folded for the children, but it is useful to show them how to do it so that they can make their own little books independently in the writing area at a later date.

Discuss what every book needs: a cover page with the title on it. Encourage all children to contribute where possible to the discussion. Explain then that the following pages will be for each stage of the lifecycle: egg/chick/hen. Demonstrate writing the title at the top of each page. Tell the children that each of the pages needs both illustration and writing on it. The writing can be as simple or complex as is necessary for your children, from a simple label, to adjectives describing the picture to simple captions with information, e.g. 'The chick is a baby hen. It is small and fluffy'.

If this is to be a guided activity…

…then the children can work together with an adult to create their own book about eggs, chicks and hens. Keep referring back to the simple non-fiction texts, drawing the children's attention to how they are different to a fiction text. If the children are able, help them to number the pages in their concertina book and construct a simple contents page to help readers find what they are looking for. Let the children test out their books on each other – can they find out about eggs? What page is the chick information on?

If this is to be an independent activity…

…then let the children attempt to make their own non-fiction books about eggs, chicks and hens. Have a variety of different colours, sizes and shapes of paper and card along with a selection of writing and drawing tools, and some methods of joining such as a stapler, tape, a hole punch and string or treasury tags. The children could make a concertina style zig-zag folded book as demonstrated in the earlier activity or they may like to design their own style of book.

To support or extend

To support, let the children make a poster about eggs, chicks and hens in a small group of two or three. Talk together about the stages in the lifecycle and decide who is going to be responsible for which part. The adult could act as scribe, writing the ideas suggested by the children. Keep reminding them of the key features of non-fiction such as title, clear illustrations, labels and captions.

To extend this activity encourage the children to write other non-fiction concertina books, with titles such as 'Pets', 'Football' or 'Food'. Explain that they can choose a subject they are interested in, and that each page should contain a different aspect of their title, e.g. 'Football' would have: kit, ball, players, goals etc. Have some simple non-fiction books for the children to look at to prompt their ideas.

Ideas for interactive display

- Have a place for the children to put up signs and information posters they have made themselves. Put out the digital camera and invite the children to use it to take photographs around the setting of information texts they have seen, for example, maybe there is a sign saying 'Please hang up your coat', or 'Take off your shoes'.

- Have a selection of non-fiction books for the children to use to look for information. Display these alongside some of the children's homemade non-fiction books.

Parents and carers as partners

At home, look at different types of information on signs, and in leaflets.
When out and about talk to your child about what the signs may mean – do they all have pictures? Try to find examples of 'No Dogs', 'No Smoking' or 'Parking'. Look together at shop windows and restaurant menus – can your child tell you about some of the information displayed?

Eggs and chicks

Egg baskets and boxes

The children will be making a simple 3D basket or box shape from a 2D net. Decorate it and put little chocolate eggs inside!

Observation and assessment

Mathematics	Expected statements (ELGs)
Shape, space and measures	Children use everyday language to talk about size, weight, capacity, position, distance, time and money to compare quantities and objects and to solve problems. They recognise, create and describe patterns. They explore characteristics of everyday objects and shapes and use mathematical language to describe them.

Key vocabulary

• shape	• glue	• corner
• cut	• 2D	• edge
• fold	• flat	• point
• bend	• 3D	• face
• stick	• solid	

Resources

★ Boxes of different sizes unfolded to create 2D nets

★ Thin card

★ 2D shapes

★ Some example nets previously photocopied onto card

★ Masking tape

★ Example of boxes and basket shapes

★ Yellow scrap paper, shredded and turned into 'straw'

★ Small chocolate eggs

★ Paper fasteners

★ Strips of card

Storybooks

★ *Egg Drop* by Mini Grey

★ *Dora's Eggs / Dora's Chicks* by Julie Sykes

What to do

Explain to the children that they are going to make a box or basket to put some small chocolate eggs inside. Show them a flat piece of card, and say that their box or basket will be made from this. Ask them how they think they can do it – encourage them to use the key vocabulary such as bend, fold, and shape. Hold up some of the unfolded cardboard boxes, plain side facing the children so that they are not distracted by the text on the box. Look at the edges and corners, faces and folds. Talk about the 2D shapes which they can see. If necessary, use differently coloured marker pens to draw around the edges (folds) of the shapes. Write the name of the shape (e.g. rectangle, square) onto the face. Then fold up the box and show the children how it moves from a flat 2D shape into a solid 3D shape.

Demonstrate sticking together with masking tape (show the children how to tear it) and talk about which face to cut off to make the opening for the box or basket. Finally talk about attaching a handle to make it into a basket using either tape or paper fasteners so that the handle will move. Add shredded yellow paper ('straw in the nest') and some small chocolate eggs. The children can decorate their construction if they wish.

If this is to be a guided activity…

…then the children can work together with an adult to create their own box or basket. Give the children a pre-drawn or printed net on thin card to cut out themselves. If you want a decorated box or basket encourage them to draw some Easter themed pictures or patterns on the side before folding and sticking their shape together.

If this is to be an independent activity…

…then show the children where the box of resources will be, and explain that they can try this activity sometime this week. Include unfolded boxes, printed nets of shapes and plain thin card for cutting and folding. Encourage the children to simply play with the resources in an open ended task – what can they make? Is it big enough/small enough? How could they make it better next time? To help them, provide shape based construction such as Polydron, Sticklebricks or Magnetix for them to play with and investigate shape informally.

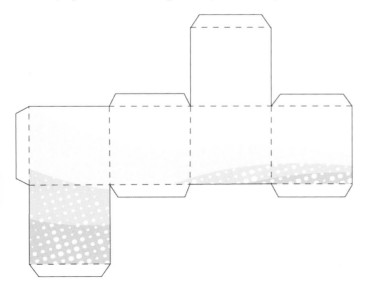

To support or extend

To support, use the unfolded cardboard boxes to make the 3D shape. They are pre-cut and pre-folded, so the children do not have to be able to use scissors accurately or fold carefully. Have a selection of different sizes available. Boxes which have contained medicines, toiletries (such as soaps) or food (such as biscuit bars or stock cubes) are all a useful size. To re-stick the boxes use masking tape, as it can be easily torn by the children to the correct length, and the papery surface is suitable for writing, colouring and painting upon. The children can then decide which flat side they would like the adult to cut off, making an open box. To make it into a basket simply help the children to make a handle from a strip of card, and either fix it with more masking tape or use a split pin/paper fastener to make a movable handle. Fill with shredded paper ('straw') and chocolate eggs.

To extend the more able children, encourage them to investigate other shapes of 3D box or container. Take apart cylinders, pyramids and prism-shaped boxes to look at which 2D shapes were necessary to form them. Help the children to recreate these shaped boxes by drawing around 2D shapes, cutting and folding. If you are having difficulty finding oddly shaped boxes or containers there are many nets of shapes available on the internet to be printed out.

Ideas for interactive display

- Put out a collection of differently shaped boxes and some sorting hoops with labels of 3D shapes. Can the children group the shapes into the correct hoop? Have some pictures of familiar objects (a tent, a wizard's hat, a dice), a box of wooden 3D shapes and some 3D shape labels. Can the children link up the correct pair? (e.g. a tent and a prism; a wizard's hat and a cone; a dice and a cube).

- Ensure there is room on the display for children to show their finished box or basket. If possible, put out some 2D nets showing the original starting point for their 3D shape – can the children pair them together?

Parents and carers as partners

At home, collect lots of old cardboard boxes and tubes – ask friends and family to collect too. Give your child a roll of masking tape: little mess, the model is ready to play with instantly, children can tear masking tape themselves safely and it can be drawn on or painted over if required. Use the names of the shapes wherever possible and let them join the boxes together to make something that interests them – e.g. a vehicle or a building. Look at their toys: would it be useful to have something to keep their Lego in, constructed from different sized boxes joined together, or to build a home for their favourite soft toy?

Eggs and chicks

Eating eggs!

The children will be looking at different ways to cook and eat eggs. They use familiar technology to cook eggs and talk about their favourites.

Observation and assessment

Understanding the world	Expected statements (ELGs)
The world	Children know about similarities and differences in relation to places, objects, materials and living things.
Technology	Children recognise that a range of technology is used in places such as homes and schools. They select and use technology for particular purposes.

Resources

* Plenty of raw eggs
* Hardboiled egg (in the shell)
* Egg cup
* Whisk
* Poaching pan
* Hob or microwave
* Bread and butter
* Range of different sorts, shapes and sizes of eggs from different birds
* Collage materials to include: yellow wool; yellow and white paper; cardboard pens and felt tips
* Pictures of ways to serve eggs: hardboiled in an egg cup; fried, scrambled; in a sandwich (search for images on the internet)

Safety first!

Check with parents and carers that children do not have egg allergies before beginning this activity. All eggs eaten by the children must be thoroughly cooked.

Storybooks

* *Meat, Fish and Eggs: (Popcorn: Good Food)* by Julia Adams
* *The Odd Egg* by Emily Gravett
* *The Easter Egg* by Jan Brett
* *Handa's Hen* by Eileen Browne

Key vocabulary

egg	white	cold
raw	scramble	slice
cook	whisk	mash
crack	beat	dip
shell	peel	spread
yolk	hot	boil

What to do

Talk to the children about eggs. What are they? Where do they come from? What do people do with them? Read some of the fiction books about eggs. Explain to the children that they are going to eat some eggs, and that they are going to try some cooked in different ways to decide upon their preference.

Show the children some eggs, including any you have from different birds. Invite the children to tell you about the way they or their families eat eggs at home. Introduce the key vocabulary, making a list on the flipchart of the different ways to cook, prepare and eat them.

Demonstrate cracking a raw egg and talk about the contents – colour, texture, feel etc. Encourage them to look closely at the egg and try to think of a word to describe it.

Have a hardboiled egg, but still in its shell so that it looks the same as the raw egg. Try cracking it – what happens? Let the children have a try. Ask them what is different about it: it is cooked. Peel the shell from the egg and slice it in half. Let the children contribute to a discussion about what it looks like now!

If it is possible to cook in front of the children do so, but if not bring them a selection of prepared eggs. Include: hardboiled with bread and butter soldiers; cold and mashed for sandwiches; scrambled; poached or fried. Encourage each child to taste a little of the eggs and say which they prefer.

If this is to be a guided activity…

…then the children can work together in a group to talk about how to prepare eggs in different ways. If possible, actually cook some eggs with the children. Talk about the different technology in the home used to cook and prepare eggs – look through a store catalogue and cut out pictures of the technology we use to store, prepare and cook eggs: hob; microwave; electric whisk; fridge. Let the children collect information on different styles of egg and display these on a poster. For example, 'Hardboiled egg' may have pictures of a hob, a pan, an egg cup, a draining spoon, a knife, a toaster and a teaspoon cut from a catalogue, and maybe some bread and butter or toast drawn on to show what it might be eaten with.

If this is to be an independent activity…

…it is very difficult for this to be a truly independent activity as it is not possible for the children to cook and eat eggs independently of an adult. However, it is possible either for the children to use ready prepared hardboiled eggs to make a filling and make sandwiches, or more likely to use paper, card and collage materials to make their own types of egg to serve up in the home corner. Chopped up yellow wool as scrambled egg; yellow and white paper fried egg; cardboard egg sandwiches can all be made to order by a waiter serving a customer choosing from a menu!

To support or extend

To support, work with a small group of children to taste the different ways of eating eggs. Have some simple pictures to show this, e.g. a boiled egg in an egg cup; a fried egg; scrambled egg and a cold hardboiled egg sandwich. Take it in turns to ask around the group which they prefer. For each preferred suggestion place a cube onto the matching picture, building small towers of different heights. This is the beginnings of a block graph. Talk to the children about which was most popular – can they remember everyone's answers? If not, would looking at the different towers of cubes tell us which was the most popular? Conversely, was there a type of egg which no-one liked?

To extend the more able children, encourage them to collect some data on people's preferred way to eat eggs and show this in a variety of ways. Prepare some simple tables for the children to complete, showing the type of egg and a simple tick, or a list of children's names and the type of egg drawn at the side. Use this data as a group to create a simple bar graph – firstly in solid form such as on an abacus or with towers of cubes, and then by transferring this data to a simple data handling programme on the computer.

Ideas for interactive display

Try to obtain a variety of different eggshells for display – include hen, duck, goose, quail or even rhea eggs, which are huge. Ask at a local farm, pet shop or children's play farm for some different types. Drain them of their contents by blowing them, and let the children look at all the different sizes, shapes, colours and texture of eggshell.

Put out some different shaped egg boxes for the children to practise counting, sorting and arrays. Include the regular 2 x 3 = 6 arrangement, but also include long strips, squares, long boxes and trays. Provide some coloured counters or cubes for the children to make patterns.

Parents and carers as partners

At home, let your child help you to prepare some eggs to eat. Talk about the different methods, and try to use words such as whisk, beat, pour, crack, cook. Wash out the shells for your child to play with; they can draw on them creatively or take them outdoors to smash into pieces in a variety of ways – a very satisfying activity.

Eggs and chicks

Chicken masks

The children will be making masks of chickens, using different yellow materials and focusing upon texture and feel of different materials.

Observation and assessment

Expressive arts and design	Expected statements (ELGs)
Exploring and using media and materials	They safely use and explore a variety of materials, tools and techniques, experimenting with colour, design, texture, form and function.
Being imaginative	Children use what they have learnt about media and materials in original ways, thinking about uses and purposes.

Key vocabulary

- beak
- feathers
- head
- eyes
- comb
- bend
- shape
- cut
- curl

Resources

★ Collage materials in 'chicken colours': yellow, white, brown, red and black

★ Feathers

★ Fabric

★ Felt

★ Paper (crêpe, tissue, sticky)

★ Card

★ Paper plate (one per child)

★ Elastic

★ Scissors

★ Stapler

★ Hole punch

★ Pictures and photographs of chickens (do an image search on the internet)

Storybooks and film clips

★ *Chick* by Ed Vere

★ *Charlie Chick* by Nick Denchfield

What to do

Explain to the children that they are going to make a mask of a chicken. They are going to use a paper plate to make the face shape and add different collage materials to show the details to make it look like a chicken. Show the children some pictures and photographs of chickens. Talk about their features – do they have big ears? What is their mouth like? Talk about the comb on top of a chicken's head – what shape is it?

Demonstrate cutting the bottom third off a paper plate to cover the children's eyes and nose, leaving their mouth clear. Talk about how to create a feathery look – if there are not enough feathers to cover each mask fully, let the children explore the different types of collage material (crêpe paper, tissue paper, sticky paper) and choose how to make it look like feathers. Encourage the children to use the key vocabulary appropriately when talking about the skills and techniques necessary. Demonstrate some paper construction techniques (curling paper, scrunching tissue, tearing crêpe paper) for the children to choose where appropriate.

Show the children how to attach elastic to each side of their plate, either by hole punching and tying, or stapling to complete their mask.

If this is to be a guided activity…

…then the children can work together with an adult to create their own mask. Guide the children with cutting and shaping the paper plate into the mask shape, helping them to move the plate with one hand when cutting with the other – this is a difficult skill. Discuss together the different types of material available for the children to use, and look at the pictures and photographs of actual chickens for ideas. Support the children to attach the elastic to their plate.

If this is to be an independent activity…

…then show the children where the box of resources will be, and explain that they can try this activity sometime this week. Put out lots of different collage materials and some plates. The plates could be pre-cut if necessary, and the elastic already attached for safety reasons. Provide the pictures and photographs of actual chickens for ideas. At the end of each day, gather the children together to say which mask looks good, and discuss the reasons why – this may give the children renewed inspiration for the following day.

To support or extend

To support, have the paper plates pre-cut into mask shapes with the elastic already attached. Have a much smaller selection of collage materials, perhaps of only one or two colours. Explain to the children that they are going to make a single colour mask, and that they are to choose, for example, all the yellow pieces of paper/feathers/fabric to attach to their mask. Talk about size, and show them how to cut a large yellow piece of paper into several smaller ones, to fit the mask.

To extend the more able children, encourage them to work independently to look carefully at other animals connected with spring to use these paper construction techniques to make another, similar mask. Can they add on tall rabbit ears, or make white curls to look like a spring lamb? Provide many collage materials and let them choose the most appropriate, giving reasons for their choices.

Ideas for interactive display

If you know anyone who has hens, enquire if they can bring one in for a while, in a pet carrier. Put it on a table in a quiet corner and let the children look and listen to it. Display the chicken masks and pictures of chickens nearby – can the children find a picture of a chicken which is the same breed?

Some companies offer an egg and incubator service: for a fee they will bring an incubator complete with fertile eggs, which hatch into chicks before the children's eyes. The children can then keep them for a little while before the chicks are homed within school or returned to the company.

Parents and carers as partners

At home, try to look at an actual animal first hand. If you, or someone you know has a pet, look carefully at it and discuss how it is similar or different to a person. How many legs does it have? Does it have hair (fur)? Touch it – how does it feel? Many pet shops have small animals such as rabbits and hamsters hopping around – look carefully how they move. Can your child move like an animal when out and about?

Spring festivals: Easter, Holi, Mardi Gras

Activity 1

The Easter story

The children will sequence the events of the Easter story correctly, retelling it accurately.

★ Simple pictures of the key events in the Easter story

★ Picture book retelling the Easter story

★ Bible

★ Flipchart/whiteboard

★ Easter artefacts: palm cross; an egg; chocolate Easter egg

★ Paper

★ Card

★ Artstraws

★ Scissors

★ Tape

Storybooks

★ *The Easter Story* by Brian Wildsmith

★ *The First Easter (Bible Story Time)* by Sophie Piper and Estelle Corke

★ *Little Bunny's Easter* by Sophie Piper and Gaby Hansen

★ *The Bunny Who Found Easter* by Charlotte Zolotow and Helen Craig

★ *Spot's First Easter* by Eric Hill

Observation and assessment

Communication and Language	Expected statements (ELGs)
Understanding	They answer 'how' and 'why' questions about their experiences and in response to stories or events.

Literacy	Expected statements (ELGs)
Reading	Children read and understand simple sentences. They use phonic knowledge to decode regular words and read them aloud accurately. They demonstrate understanding when talking with others about what they have read.

Key vocabulary

Jesus	Good Friday	boulder
Son of God	Easter Sunday	friends
died	tomb	soldiers
cross	stone	

What to do

Talk to the children about Easter. What do they already know about this festival? Collect their ideas and draw/write them onto a flipchart or whiteboard. Discuss the real meaning of Easter – do they know any of the Easter story? Explain that Christians believe that Easter is the time when Jesus died and came back to life again, and that this is a special belief, but that it is not possible for anyone else to die and come back to life. Use the key vocabulary when looking at the picture book. Hold up the Bible, introduce this as an artefact that has special significance to Christians as it is where all the stories about Jesus are written down.

Ensure that the children know the key events in the story. Check by asking a few questions, for example 'What happened first? Who went to look for Jesus' body in the tomb?'

Show the children the sequencing pictures and demonstrate putting them in order. Make an intentional mistake, and show the children how to check the ordered pictures for accuracy and rectify any errors in the sequence. Encourage all children to contribute where possible.

If this is to be a guided activity…

…then the children can work together with an adult to put their own set of pictures in the correct order. Provide strips of paper for the children to glue their pictures on to. Type up simple captions to match each picture. Read these to the children, asking them to pair up the corresponding picture and caption.

If this is to be an independent activity…

…then show the children where the pictures for sequencing are and some matching captions. Provide some of the Easter storybooks that you looked at together for the children to look at for support and ideas. Let the children work in a small team to sequence the pictures and, if possible, match the captions. Give them some Blu-tack to put the pictures on a flipchart to show the rest of the class. Discuss the outcome in a plenary session – did they get it all correct?

To support or extend

To support, look at the story of Easter together using a simple book with clear illustrations. Draw the children's attention to the key parts of the story, asking questions to ensure they understand what happened. Explain that this story is part of the celebration of Easter, a Christian festival. Show the children the artefacts including the egg and the chocolate egg. Explain that the egg contains new life in the form of a chick, and that we have eggs at Easter to remind us of the new life of Jesus Christ.

To extend the more able children, encourage them to look at the artefacts related to Easter. Explain that when Jesus came to visit the people they were so pleased to see him that they put down palm leaves on the floor for his donkey to walk across, making a special pathway for him. Try to show them a palm leaf (even if it is from a type of house plant). Talk about the narrow fronds, and show them a palm cross. Explain the symbolism behind the shape – it is to represent the cross that Jesus died upon. Using materials from the classroom (paper, card, art straws) let the children investigate making their own cross. Ensure that they know the sequence of the Easter Story and the relevance of the palm leaves for Palm Sunday.

Ideas for interactive display

- Make an 'Easter table' where many artefacts can be displayed. Put up pictures of animals associated with Easter such as hens, chicks and rabbits. Encourage the children to bring in any Easter artefacts they may have, for example the packaging from their Easter eggs, or Easter storybooks.

- Have a palm cross on display with the Easter storybooks. Provide art straws, scissors and tape – can the children make their own?

Parents and carers as partners

At home, talk about signs of Easter. When out and about look for signs of Easter celebrations in the shops – Easter eggs, hot cross buns, pictures of rabbits and chicks. If you visit a church look for palm crosses on display, and notice the new life in spring plants as the weather becomes warmer.

Spring festivals: Easter, Holi, Mardi Gras

Pancake maths

The children will be reading, writing and using a recipe for pancakes to make enough pancakes for everyone to share!

Observation and assessment

Mathematics	Expected statements (ELGs)
Numbers	Children count reliably with numbers from 1 to 20, place them in order and say which number is one more or one less than a given number. They solve problems, including doubling, halving and sharing.
Shape, space and measures	Children use everyday language to talk about size, weight, capacity, position, distance, time and money to compare quantities and objects and to solve problems.

Resources

★ Simple recipe for pancakes

★ Pancake ingredients: milk, plain flour, eggs and butter

★ Mixing bowl

★ Sieve

★ Whisk or fork

★ Non-stick pan

★ Weighing scales

★ Hob

★ Toppings for the pancakes: squeezed orange and lemon, sugar, treacle or jam, chocolate spread

★ Ingredients to make salt dough: flour, water, salt

★ Wooden spoons

★ Rolling pins

Safety first! Ensure that none of the children have allergies to any of the foods being prepared or eaten.

Storybooks

★ *Pancakes, Pancakes!* by Eric Carle

★ *Mr Wolf's Pancakes* by Jan Fearnley

★ *Shrove Tuesday, Ash Wednesday and Mardi Gras: (Living Festivals)* by Margaret Davidson

Key vocabulary

- pancake
- cook
- stir
- mix
- pour
- measure
- weigh
- more
- less
- enough
- the same
- bigger
- smaller

What to do

Explain to the children that traditionally pancakes are eaten all around the world before Easter, at the beginning of a period called Lent. People use up the ingredients left in their cupboards by making pancakes before beginning a period of fasting for 40 days. This is symbolic of Jesus' time lost in the wilderness. Read *Mr Wolf's Pancakes*.

Look at how pancakes are made, and the ingredients needed. Show the children the ingredients, introducing the key vocabulary where relevant. Tell them that they are going to help you make some pancakes, firstly by sieving the flour into the mixing bowl, adding the other ingredients and whisking into a batter, cooking in the pan and then by choosing different toppings when they have been cooked on a stove by an adult.

Show the children the simple recipe, if possible, reproduce it on a large sheet so all children can see it on the flipchart. Discuss the purpose behind a recipe, and draw the children's attention to the key features: the numbered steps in the sequence, the weights, measures and timings.

Demonstrate how to use the scales by weighing the first ingredient. Encourage children to come up and help with the measuring, weighing and mixing until the batter is made.

When the pancakes are made, prepare some with different toppings and let the children try a few. Talk together as a group to find out which was most liked. This activity can lead to a follow up mathematics lesson; by creating a simple pictograph or bar chart the children can contribute to some simple data handling.

If this is to be a guided activity…

…then the children can work together with an adult to weigh, measure and mix the ingredients into a batter. When the batter has been cooked bring the pancakes back to the children. Ideally, cook the pancakes in front of the children so that they can watch or help to flip them.

If this is to be an independent activity…

…cooking pancakes cannot be an entirely independent activity due to the safety risks involved with children and cooking. However, there are many simple foods children could make independently by following a simple recipe sheet such as sandwiches, milkshake or fruit salad.

To support or extend

To support, make the pancakes prior to working with the children. Show them the finished pancakes and explain that the children are going to help you choose and prepare different toppings, before eating them and saying which they liked the most. Encourage the children to think of a topping they may have eaten before; if not on pancakes, then on toast. Have popular choices to hand so that the children can spread jam, honey or chocolate spread onto some pancakes, as well as some fruit such as oranges and lemons (or carton pure juice to pour onto the pancake). When they have tried some different pancakes invite them to talk about their favourite. If they have tried a new taste, congratulate them.

To extend this activity, provide a simple laminated recipe for making cold salt dough. Put the ingredients into a large sand tray along with a mixing bowl and wooden spoons. Let the children try to make their own piece of salt dough by following the simple recipe. The ingredients can be measured in cups and half cups to simplify the weighing and measuring if necessary.

Ideas for interactive display

Put out some play dough, rolling pins and differently-sized pans. Encourage the children to practise rolling out differently-sized balls of play dough to make circular pancakes to fit the different pans. Outdoors, provide beans bags and flat table tennis style bats for the children to play running races whilst carrying their 'pancake'.

Parents and carers as partners

At home, make some pancakes together. Let your child be involved at each stage so that they can see the changes from separate ingredients into one wet liquid batter. Try out different toppings on the pancake, sweet and savoury – which one does your child prefer? Talk to family and friends to find out how they like to eat their pancakes.

Spring festivals: Easter, Holi, Mardi Gras

Activity 3

Holi traditions

The children will be looking at the festival of Holi and how it is celebrated in other countries. The children can throw confetti, powder paint or squirt water outdoors whilst wearing their old clothes!

Resources

★ Outdoor space

★ Old clothes for the children to wear

★ Powder paint /coloured flour

★ Coloured water in squeezy bottles

★ Collection of water pistols, watering cans, syringes and squeezy bottles

★ Confetti and paper streamers

★ Huge piece of paper (or several strips of wall lining paper taped together), laid on the floor outdoors

★ Coloured paint mixed to a runny consistency

★ Examples of abstract artwork by Jackson Pollock (do an image search on the internet)

Storybooks

★ *Holi (Celebrations in My World)* by Lynn Peppas

★ *Celebrating Holi: A Hindu Celebration of Spring (We Love Holidays)* by Sujatha Menon

Observation and assessment

Understanding the world	Expected statements (ELGs)
The world	Children talk about past and present events in their own lives and the lives of family members. They know that other children don't always enjoy the same things and are sensitive to this. They know about similarities and differences between themselves and others, and among families, communities and traditions.

Key vocabulary

- Holi
- Hindu
- Krishna
- Holika
- Prahlad
- celebration
- powder paint
- coloured water
- squirt
- splash
- drip
- drop
- flick
- squeeze

What to do

Explain to the children they are going to look at a celebration held in North India by people who follow Hindu faith and traditions. It is usually held in March to celebrate the coming of spring. Some families hold religious ceremonies but for many Holi is a time for fun and mischievousness.

Holi is a colourful festival with dancing, singing and special food. All ages of the family join in, throwing coloured water and powder paint at each other. Show some photographs of the celebration to the children. Explain that the traditional stories told at Holi symbolise good overcoming evil.

Explain to the children (and in advance to parents/carers) that this will be a very messy activity and that they need to wear old clothes that may be spoiled by paint. Look at some of the photographs in the books of people splashed with powder paint. Explain that they are going to mix the powder paint with water to make a paler, watery variety to play with. Ask the children what would be the best way to splash paint onto someone else? Show them the squeezy bottles, syringes, watering cans and water pistols, and introduce the key vocabulary. Explain that they are going to go outdoors where they can make a mess (on the grass at a park, in a field, in an open space) and have fun covering each other in coloured watery paint. Remain sensitive to any children who do not enjoy messy activities and let them squirt each other's hands to begin with.

If you do not have a messy outdoor area simply use water for the activity which will quickly dry outside.

If you have only an inside space, then replace the paint and water with brightly coloured confetti, pieces of flimsy fabric or paper streamers which the children can throw at each other and play with.

If this is to be a guided activity…

…then the children can work together with an adult to create a large picture in the style of Jackson Pollock (1912-1956) an American artist who used liquid paint in a variety of ways including dripping, pouring and flicking to create large pieces of abstract art. Search the internet and show the children some examples of his 'action painting'. Preferably outdoors, take the children to the large piece of paper taped to the ground. Provide them with a variety of equipment to create their own artwork. Discuss how Pollock rarely used the traditional artists' tools of brushes, palettes and easel and let the children choose their own method of applying paint to the paper on the floor.

If this is to be an independent activity…

…then show the children where the messy table resources are and explain that they can try this activity sometime this week. Put out powder paint and water, and encourage the children to attempt paint mixing, looking at the different textures they achieve. The children may need a demonstration first, but then let them independently explore the properties of the paint they mix, ideally to a runny consistency which can be flicked, dripped or squirted onto paper. If the area is suitable provide small syringes and straws for the children to apply it to the paper in a variety of ways.

To support or extend

To support, take the children outside and let them play with water. Give them a variety of materials to 'paint' with, from small toothbrushes to the adult sweeping brush. Wall papering brushes and dustpan brushes are also fun. This activity works best if the ground is dry. As the children 'paint' with the water it leaves a mark on the ground. Encourage them to practise making marks in different ways, or to make the longest line they can. As the marks are drying in the sun it is fun to run and jump on the lines and splashes made until they are all gone.

To extend the more able children by encouraging them to create their own artwork in the style of Jackson Pollock. Look together at some of his work, talking about the colours he chose. Did he use every colour available, or choose similar colours such as blues and purples, or yellows and oranges? Help the children to mix their own watery paint from powder paint, and then drip the different colours onto their paper.

Ideas for interactive display

- Display large pictures of people celebrating Holi. If you have any Hindu children in your setting encourage them to bring in any photographs or resources from home to add to the display. Enquire whether there is a family member with direct experience of celebrating Holi who would be able to come in and talk to the children.

- If the display is indoors include clean, dry, colourful items to represent the coloured water, such as confetti, paper streamers or coloured rice. Make a small world scene in the sand tray with the dolls' house people and let the children recreate their experience from outdoors.

Parents and carers as partners

At home, take your child to an outdoor space and let them experiment playing with water. On a sunny day it is possible to 'paint' with a brush and water onto the floor and wall surfaces, and then let the sun simply dry it out. If you have a selection of differently-sized brushes (paintbrush, toothbrush, sweeping brush) then your child can experiment making a variety of marks on different scales. Encourage your child to attempt some of the letters in their name, or take it in turns to copy what the other has drawn.

Spring festivals: Easter, Holi, Mardi Gras

Mardi Gras musical instruments

The children will be making a musical instrument to play at the Mardi Gras festival parade.

Observation and assessment

Expressive arts and design	Expected statements (ELGs)
Exploring and using media and materials	Children sing songs, make music and dance and experiment with ways of changing them.
Being imaginative	They represent their own ideas, thoughts and feelings through design and technology, art, music, dance, role-play and stories.

Resources

★ Percussion instruments: shakers, maracas, castanets, bells, triangles, tambourines, tambours and drums

★ Stringed instrument such as a guitar or banjo

★ Film clip of a Mardi Gras or carnival parade (look on the internet for a news clip of the Notting Hill Carnival or New Orleans Mardi Gras)

★ Boxes

★ Cans

★ Packaging

★ Elastic bands

★ Dried beans/peas/lentils

★ Colourful scarves and drapes

Storybooks and film clips

★ *Dinosaur Mardi Gras* by Dianne de las Casas

★ *Gaston Goes to Mardi Gras* by James Rice

★ *Jenny Giraffe's Mardi Gras Ride* by Cecilia Casrill Dartez

★ *Mardi Gras and Carnival: (Celebrations In My World)* by Molly Aloian

Key vocabulary

- shake
- rattle
- click
- tap
- bang
- jingle
- hit
- shaker
- maracas
- castanets
- bells
- triangle
- tambour
- tambourine
- drum
- guitar
- strings
- pluck

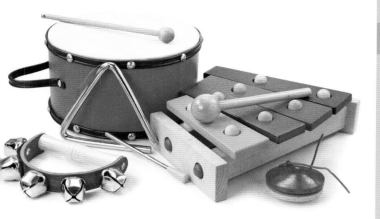

What to do

Explain to the children that they are going to make a musical instrument to play in a musical parade. Show them the filmclip of Rio Carnival or Mardi Gras parade. Talk about the sights, sounds and people they can see – note the instruments, the music and the people dancing. Remind the children about Pancake Day and the reason for celebrating it: to use up fats and sugars in the house before Lent (traditionally a period of fasting) begins. The literal translation of 'Mardi Gras' is Fat Tuesday, and the reason for the celebration is the same.

Demonstrate how the percussion instruments work. Let all the children play with the different instruments, and then together support the children to group the instruments how they see fit. Make this a collaborative activity, and use questioning to discover why some instruments are grouped together – it may be the shape, method of playing, material they are made from or the sound they make.

Encourage the children to use the correct vocabulary when sorting or grouping the instruments, e.g. 'I have put the maracas with the shakers because they both make a rattling sound'.

Show the children any larger instruments (e.g. the guitar) how they are played. If it is possible to find a musician to give a demonstration the children will be enthralled.

If this is to be a guided activity…

…then the children can work together with an adult to identify the type of instrument they would like to make. Explain that they are allowed to choose any of the junk modelling boxes they like to make a working model of an instrument. The adult may need to demonstrate, for example by putting elastic bands over a tissue box to make a 'guitar', or by filling an empty plastic bottle with dried peas to make a 'maraca'. These instruments can be decorated after construction.

If this is to be an independent activity…

…then show the children where the box of resources will be, and explain that they can try this activity sometime this week. Model some of the simple techniques necessary for making a junk instrument, e.g. putting rice in a tub and sealing the lid, or stretching plastic over a box to make a 'drum', but let the children use their own imaginations when designing and making their instruments. Encourage them to decorate it when it is completed.

To support, limit the children to a simple shaker type instrument so that they do not have to make as many choices when designing and making it. For example, simply provide a range of containers with lids, and a range of dried pulses or rice to be the 'beads' inside. Encourage the children to say why they are choosing a particular container: 'It is easy to hold', 'It's the biggest!' and also why they have chosen, say, rice instead of beans: 'It makes a swooshier sound'. Encourage the use of correct vocabulary wherever possible.

To extend the more able children, encourage them to work independently to use a limited range of resources to focus upon making only one type of instrument, e.g. a shaker. Try to investigate, for example, which filling would make the loudest rattle, or the gentlest sound. Discuss the idea of a fair test and variables in testing – explain that if the inside material is going to change then the exterior container needs to be made of the same material each time for comparison purposes. Together, devise a method of testing their predictions and carry out a fair test. Were they correct in their assumptions?

Ideas for interactive display

- Display some photographs of Carnival or Mardi Gras showing people dressed in costume or in brightly coloured masks and clothing. Provide some dressing-up scarves, masks and hats for the children to wear and move around in.

- Set up a CD player which the children are allowed to use with a carnival style CD. Tell the children that they can play the music and have their own parade any time!

- Make a space to display the existing percussion instruments as well as those made by the children. Put up clear pictures of well-known percussion instruments with simple name labels attached. Explain to the children that they can use any of the instruments to make music, but that they are all precious and must be treated with respect.

Parents and carers as partners

At home, make simple rattles, shakers and drums from junk boxes, tubs, pots and bottles. A simple shaker is easily made from a plastic bottle with a screw lid containing a handful of dried peas or rice. Bottles of different sizes could be used, e.g. a tiny food colouring bottle, a small water bottle and a large fizzy drink bottle. Compare the sounds they make – be a family 'band' and parade around your home or outdoors!

Spring parade!

Celebrating spring!

The final week of the topic is an opportunity to invite parents and carers into the setting to share some of the activities in which the children have been involved over the preceeding five weeks.

Tickell stated in her review that,

'Where parents and carers are actively encouraged to participate confidently in their children's learning and healthy development, the outcomes for children will be at their best'

It is crucial that parents and carers are involved and feel able to support their children at every stage of development. This final week is, therefore, a time for the children to celebrate their successes, perform some of their new skills for their families to see and for parents and carers to be involved in their learning.

In the week building up to inviting the parents and carers into the setting the children can be involved in making invitations, decorations, food and practising songs, drama and dances to share on the special day.

The actual event can be really flexible in length, style and amount of parental involvement. Depending on the setting and the number of children involved it is possible to make this event an hour or a day long, or you may need to repeat it for two different cohorts of children. It could simply be an open style morning or afternoon for people to drop in, to look at things the children have made, or be a mini concert, where the children can perform dances, sing songs for the parents and afterwards share food the children have produced.

Whatever the design, the purpose is to share some of the activities and crafts the children have been involved in, and to celebrate the topic of spring.

Listed below are ideas for celebration linked to each of the seven areas of learning, along with some ideas for parental involvement and understanding. The detailed expected ELG is also noted again here as a reminder of the expected level of attainment and understanding.

These are just some of the possible ideas – have fun, be creative and do whatever works for you and your children.

Ideas for a spring parade

- Make invitations, cards and decorations – invitations to the carnival parade, make animal masks, Easter bonnets or strings of spring flowers to wear.

- Decorate the setting with some of the artwork produced – display the moving animal pictures and chicken masks; have a spring blossom corner and display the Japanese style paintings alongside some actual blossom.

- Eat special food – make some chocolate crispy egg nests from cereals, and pancakes to share with the parents and carers, or cook some eggs in different ways to find out the guests' preferences.

- Dress up in special clothing – allow the children to wear their best party clothes, or spring related fancy dress, or traditional Hindu clothing to celebrate Holi; decorate the children's faces with Easter eggs painted onto their cheeks.

- Play party games – move like a jumping frog, a leaping rabbit or a springing lamb; listen to some traditional Mardi Gras carnival parade music and march around with some home-made instruments; wear Easter bonnets or hats and parade around the setting.

Opportunities within Literacy

Aspect	Expected statements (ELGs)
Reading	Children read and understand simple sentences. They use phonic knowledge to decode regular words and read them aloud accurately. They also read some common irregular words. They demonstrate understanding when talking with others about what they have read.
Writing	Children use their phonic knowledge to write words in ways which match their spoken sounds. They also write some irregular common words. They write simple sentences which can be read by themselves and others. Some words are spelt correctly and others are phonetically plausible.

Most parents and carers are used to and comfortable with sharing books with children, as it is something that they have enjoyed regularly at home as their child has grown up. It's therefore a good idea to set up a corner within the setting with cushions, low tables and chairs to invite adults to sit quietly with the children reading, talking and listening. Put out a selection of books related to the topics, particularly including books that the children have seen before and which they have enjoyed in the setting. Include both fiction and non-fiction to appeal to a wide range of children and adults, and also include dual language texts. The children will relish being the expert when sharing the books with their parent or carer, and it gives a little quiet time to those finding the celebration a little busy.

Put out a writing area with a variety of suitable materials – include sticky labels, coloured sticky notes, postcards, envelopes, folded pieces of paper, lined, squared and dotted paper, old birthday or Christmas cards, old diaries and calendars and anything else the children would like to write upon! Include a mixture of pens, pencils and crayons. In this area also include blank invitations, Easter and Holi cards and spring pictures to colour, cut and stick – the children and adults can have fun writing to each other and making cards or invitations. Children then see writing as having a purpose. If there are a variety of materials which are easily found in a home setting it may also give ideas to adults to encourage them to provide similar writing opportunities at home.

Opportunities within Mathematics

Aspect	Expected statements (ELGs)
Numbers	Children count reliably with numbers from 1 to 20, place them in order and say which number is one more or one less than a given number. Using quantities and objects, they add and subtract two single-digit numbers and count on or back to find the answer. They solve problems, including doubling, halving and sharing.
Space, shape and measures	Children use everyday language to talk about size, weight, capacity, position, distance, time and money to compare quantities and objects and to solve problems. They recognise, create and describe patterns. They explore characteristics of everyday objects and shapes and use mathematical language to describe them.

Let the children prepare for the adults visiting the setting by working out how many things will be needed for example: how many chairs altogether; how many around each table; how many cups or plates are needed? Setting the tables: have we enough; how many more; are they the same/equal? Extend this idea to the preparation of food when weighing or measuring quantities for making pancakes and chocolate cereal egg nests, or when buttering and cutting bread for egg sandwiches.

Have a basket of pennies for the parents to 'spend' when they are buying a cake or a pancake – can they help the children to count accurately?

Remind the children of the work they did on 2D and 3D shape, using nets to make boxes. Put out some more nets with the wooden building shapes – can they use the different nets to make more solid shapes? Tell the children that they are to teach the adults how to do it. Ensure that there are clearly labelled pictures of the shapes and their names to encourage the visiting adults to use the correct vocabulary.

These ideas are easily replicated at home, and the parents and carers can see how easy it is to provide simple mathematical activities at home without any special books or mathematical equipment.

Opportunities within Understanding the world

Aspect	Expected statements (ELGs)
People and communities	Children talk about past and present events in their own lives and in the lives of family members. They know that other children don't always enjoy the same things, and are sensitive to this. They know about similarities and differences between themselves and others, and among families, communities and traditions.
The world	Children know about similarities and differences in relation to places, objects, materials and living things. They talk about the features of their own immediate environment and how environments might vary from one another. They make observations of animals and plants and explain why some things occur, and talk about changes.
Technology	Children recognise that a range of technology is used in places such as homes and schools. They select and use technology for particular purposes.

Make a display of the photographs taken during the Holi celebrations and pancake making. The children will enjoy talking about the 'messy day', and if there are some simple non-fiction books available the children can explain to their parent or carer a little about these festivals.

The use of ICT in the setting may be the most surprising to the parent and carer visitors. Ensure the computers and whiteboard are on (if you have them), digital cameras and voice recorders are available to use and toys such as programmable toys and pretend telephones and ovens are out for the children to show to the adults. Many parents and carers will believe that ICT relates only to computers: this is an opportunity to show them that technology includes the common objects in their own home.

A very simple but effective idea is to put all the photographs you have taken over the previous five weeks on as a slideshow – the children will love pointing themselves out, it is good evidence of the type of activities the children have been involved in and it will naturally prompt talk, listening and laughter.

Opportunities within Expressive arts and design

Aspect	Expected statements (ELGs)
Exploring and using media and materials	Children sing songs, make music and dance, and experiment with ways of changing them. They safely use and explore a variety of materials, tools and techniques, experimenting with colour, design, texture, form and function.
Being imaginative	Children use what they have learnt about media and materials in original ways, thinking about uses and purposes. They represent their own ideas, thoughts and feelings through design and technology, art, music, dance, role-play and stories.

Have an area set out as a place where adults and children can work together to produce decorations and artwork relevant to the topics looked at over the preceding five weeks. Provide paints for colour mixing to let the children show off their skills; put the chalks outside for the children to draw rainbows on the floor; or provide brushes and water for the children to 'write' with outside on the ground. Simple pictures to colour (e.g. spring flowers, carnival parades or Easter egg patterns) is also a popular activity which many adults are comfortable with, and may choose to sit alongside children and participate in without any fear of 'doing it wrong'.

If your setting allows for it, prepare an area with some musical instruments (include both those made by the children and existing ones) and possibly a CD player with some traditional Mardi Gras carnival parade music. Let the children play the CD and investigate playing the instruments alongside. This activity works well outdoors, as there is more space for the children to march and move with the instruments. The increased space may also enable children to feel 'free' and you may find that they initiate an entire parade, making music and marching in time to the music! If you extend their opportunities by also providing coloured scarves, fabric and masks they are also more likely to develop characters within the music and begin to role-play quite naturally. Parents and carers can see from this that expensive character fancy dress sets are not necessary - with only a couple of old hats and scarves they can provide valuable opportunities at home for dressing up and firing their children's imagination.

Opportunities within Communication and language

Aspect	Expected statements (ELGs)
Listening and attention	Children listen attentively in a range of situations. They listen to stories, accurately anticipating key events and respond to what they hear with relevant comments, questions or actions. They give their attention to what others say and respond appropriately, while engaged in another activity.
Understanding	Children follow instructions involving several ideas or actions. They answer 'how' and 'why' questions about their experiences and in response to stories or events.
Speaking	Children express themselves effectively, showing awareness of listeners' needs. They use past, present and future forms accurately when talking about events that have happened or are to happen in the future. They develop their own narratives and explanations by connecting ideas or events.

For some children who can find the setting a little overwhelming sharing their activities and successes with a familiar adult can be reassuring. They appreciate the time to be the expert, talking to their parent or carer about their daily activities and routines without the pressure to chat to a stranger or in front of others. For the practitioner in the setting this is also an ideal opportunity to listen quietly and unobtrusively to the child's conversation with others – it may be the first time you have heard the child speak!

Opportunities within Physical development

Aspect	Expected statements (ELGs)
Moving and handling	Children show good control and co-ordination in large and small movements. They move confidently in a range of ways, safely negotiating space. They handle equipment and tools effectively, including pencils for writing.
Health and self-care	Children know the importance for good health of physical exercise, and a healthy diet, and talk about ways to keep healthy and safe. They manage their own basic hygiene and personal needs successfully, including dressing and going to the toilet independently.

This can link quite closely with the music and movement idea in Expressive arts and design, where the children can move confidently and with control around the outdoor environment. It is useful for the parents and carers to note that young children need to have opportunities for physical play or movement several times a day, whether it is walking to school or running around the local park or garden.

There are many activities which encourage fine motor skills, including threading bead patterns; making rainbows with coloured pegs and peg boards; building with construction or using pencils to trace, write, draw and colour. Parents can extend this at home very simply without any special equipment, for example by threading penne pasta onto string to make jewellery, using clothes pegs to hang out the washing; playing with small construction (e.g. Lego) or small world (e.g. a doll's house) or cutting pieces of baking paper for children to place over the pictures in their colouring book to use as a cheap alternative to tracing paper. It is vital that parents recognise these pre-writing skills as crucial in a child's fine motor development.

To promote good health and self-care it is useful to have a large display where the children (but more importantly, the parents and carers) can see it, showing which children can achieve such things as using the toilet independently, washing their hands, putting on their own coat or fastening their own shoes. Maybe have small photographs of each child, and when they have achieved the target then their photograph is moved onto, for example, a large outline of a coat. The children in the setting will then be very aware of what they need to do, and will take this information home in the form of pester power – quickly learning how to perform the skill! Sometimes parents and carers do not realise what is necessary for their child to become more independent.

Opportunities within Personal, social and emotional development

Aspect	Expected statements (ELGs)
Self-confidence and self-awareness	Children are confident to try new activities, and say why they like some activities more than others. They are confident to speak in a familiar group, will talk about their ideas, and will choose the resources they need for their chosen activities. They say when they do or don't need help.
Managing feelings and behaviour	Children talk about how they and others show feelings, talk about their own and others' behaviour, and its consequences, and know that some behaviour is unacceptable. They work as part of a group or class, and understand and follow the rules. They adjust their behaviour to different situations, and take changes of routine in their stride.
Making relationships	Children play co-operatively, taking turns with others. They take account of one another's ideas about how to organise their activity. They show sensitivity to others' needs and feelings, and form positive relationships with adults and other children.

Within the six week topic block there are continual opportunities for children to demonstrate their development in the aspect of PSED. Each activity throughout the previous weeks requires children to work together, co-operate, talk about their ideas, choose resources and form positive relationships with others. This final opportunity for celebration allows the children to show that this positive behaviour is embedded, as the key skill of adjusting their behaviour to different situations and taking changes in routine in their stride is certainly tested during this busy week.

Make a note of any children who have struggled with certain aspects of PSED and ensure that they are prepared for this change in routine: pair them with a particular friend for security; provide them with a quiet space (e.g. a tent, a book corner, even another room in the setting with another group) to which they can escape when it becomes too much; give them a key responsibility to prevent idle hands (such as handing out biscuits to adults, collecting empty cups or even tidying pencils and putting away chairs) or simply ensure that they are your 'special helper' and that they are to stay with you throughout the event. This way you are building on the personal, social and emotional capabilities of your children and allowing them to develop further within a safe and structured environment.

Ensure most importantly that parents and carers understand the uniqueness of each child. Measuring their child's attainment, progress and temperament against that of another child is of no benefit whatsoever. A child who feels loved, supported and a valuable member of their early years community will grow and develop into an adult that is able to love and support others, and more importantly will be a valuable member of any community they choose to belong to throughout the rest of their life.

Observation record: Characteristics of Effective Learning

Name: _____ DoB: _____

Characteristics	Date	Activity observed	Evidence (What did you see?)
Playing and Exploring • Finding out and exploring • Playing with what they know • Being willing to 'have a go'			
Through active learning • Being involved and concentrating • Keeping trying • Enjoying achieving what they set out to do			
By creating and thinking critically • Having their own ideas • Making links • Choosing ways to do things			

Group record sheet for Communication and language (**prime**) and Literacy (**specific**)

Date completed _____

Children's names	Communication and language (prime)						Literacy (specific)				
	Listening and attention		Understanding		Speaking		Reading			Writing	

Group record sheet for **prime** areas of learning (Personal, social and emotional development and Physical development)   Date completed _____

Children's names	Personal, social and emotional development (prime)									Physical development (prime)						
	Self-confidence and self-awareness			Managing feelings and behaviour			Making relationships			Moving and handling			Health and self-care		

Creative Planning in the EYFS © Lucy Peet

Group record sheet for **specific** area of learning (Mathematics)

Children's names	Mathematics (specific)					Comments
	Numbers			Shape, space and measures		

Group record sheet for **specific** areas of learning (Understanding the world and Expressive arts and design)

Date completed _____

Children's names	People and communities			The world			Technology			Exploring and using media and materials			Being imaginative		

Understanding the world (specific)

Expressive arts and design (specific)

Planning overview: Spring (weeks 1-2)

Week	Main topic and activities	ELGs covered from specific areas of learning			
		Literacy including some communication and language	Mathematics	Understanding the world	Expressive arts and design
1	**Rain or shine** • Sing a rainbow! • Rainbow arches and bridges • Making rainbows! • Rainbow displays	Learn to sing 'I can sing a rainbow', signing the colours using Makaton or BSL. Make a simple picture sequence. Children listen attentively in a range of situations. They give their attention to what others say and respond appropriately, while engaged in another activity. Children use their phonic knowledge to write words in ways which match their spoken sounds. They also write some irregular common words. They write simple sentences which can be read by themselves and others. Some words are spelt correctly and others are phonetically plausible.	Look at curves and arches. Use vocabulary from shape and space, and build arches and bridges with construction. Children count reliably with numbers from 1 to 20, place them in order and say which number is one more or one less than a given number. They solve problems, including doubling, halving and sharing. Children use everyday language to talk about size, weight, capacity, position, distance, time and money to compare quantities and objects and to solve problems. They recognise, create and describe patterns.	Make a rainbow outside on a sunny day by spraying a hosepipe, looking how the sunlight shines through the rain. Children know about similarities and differences in relation to places, objects, materials and living things. They make observations of animals and plants and explain why some things occur, and talk about changes. Children recognise that a range of technology is used in places such as homes and schools. They select and use technology for particular purposes.	Have a 'rainbow week' wearing a different colour each day, and using craft and collage materials in the colour of the day. They safely use and explore a variety of materials, tools and techniques, experimenting with colour, design, texture, form and function. Children use what they have learnt about media and materials in original ways, thinking about uses and purposes. They represent their own ideas, thoughts and feelings through design and technology, art, music, dance, role-play and stories.
2	**Hop, skip and jump** • Peter Rabbit's new friend • Jumping numbers • Paper plate lifecycles. • Wagging tails, floppy ears and jumping legs	Read some of Beatrix Potter's Peter Rabbit stories, look at the characters and make up a new character. Children read and understand simple sentences. They use phonic knowledge to decode regular words and read them aloud accurately. They demonstrate understanding when talking with others about what they have read. They develop their own narratives and explanations by connecting ideas or events.	Use number lines to practice counting forwards and backwards. Extend to counting in multiples of two, five and ten. Children count reliably with numbers from 1 to 20, place them in order and say which number is one more or one less than a given number. They solve problems, including doubling, halving and sharing. Children use everyday language to talk about size, weight, capacity, position, distance, time and money to compare quantities and objects and to solve problems. They recognise, create and describe patterns.	Sequence the stages in the lifecycle of a frog, and decorate a paper plate to show it. Children know about similarities and differences in relation to places, objects, materials and living things. They make observations of animals and plants and explain why some things occur, and talk about changes.	Make a moving picture from card, with a wagging lamb's tail, floppy rabbit ears and jumping frog legs. They safely use and explore a variety of materials, tools and techniques, experimenting with colour, design, texture, form and function. Children use what they have learnt about media and materials in purposeful and original ways. They represent their own ideas, thoughts and feelings through art and design, music, dance, role-play and stories.

Planning overview: Spring (weeks 3 - 4)

Week	Main topic and activities	ELGs covered from specific areas of learning			
		Literacy including some communication and language	Mathematics	Understanding the world	Expressive arts and design
3	**Blooming blossoms** · How to plant a bulb · Pennies and flowers: how much? · Growing cress heads · Japanese blow painting	Write simple instructions on how to plant a bulb in a flowerpot. Children use their phonic knowledge to write words in ways which match their spoken sounds. They also write some irregular common words. They write simple sentences which can be read by themselves and others. Some words are spelt correctly and others are phonetically plausible.	Using 1p and 2p coins to make flower additions. Children use everyday language to talk about size, weight, capacity, position, distance, time and money to compare quantities and objects and to solve problems.	Growing cress in an eggshell. Extend to growing grass seed to make a small environment. Children know about similarities and differences in relation to places, objects, materials and living things. They talk about the features of their own immediate environment and how environments might vary from one another. They make observations of animals and plants and explain why some things occur, and talk about changes.	Blowing paint through a straw to make a twig background. Adding finger prints in pinks and white to represent flower blossom. They safely use and explore a variety of materials, tools and techniques, experimenting with colour, design, texture, form and function. Children use what they have learnt about media and materials in original ways, thinking about uses and purposes. They represent their own ideas, thoughts and feelings through design and technology, art, music, dance, role-play and stories.
4	**Eggs and chicks** · Zig-zag book: from egg to hen · Egg baskets and boxes · Eating eggs · Chicken masks	Make a simple folded book showing the development of an egg into a hen. Children listen attentively in a range of situations. They listen to stories, accurately anticipating key events and respond to what they hear with relevant comments, questions or actions. They can give their attention to what others say and respond appropriately, while engaged in another activity.. Children use their phonic knowledge to write words in ways which match their spoken sounds. They also write some irregular common words.	Make a simple 3D basket or box from a 2D net. Decorate it and put little chocolate eggs inside! Children use everyday language to talk about size, weight, capacity, position, distance, time and money to compare quantities and objects and to solve problems. They recognise, create and describe patterns. They explore characteristics of everyday objects and shapes and use mathematical language to describe them.	Look at different ways to cook and eat eggs. Use familiar technology to cook eggs and talk about their favourites. Children know about similarities and differences in relation to places, objects, materials and living things Children recognise that a range of technology is used in places such as homes and schools. They select and use technology for particular purposes.	Make a mask of a chicken from a paper plate, decorating it with feathers and curled yellow paper. They safely use and explore a variety of materials, tools and techniques, experimenting with colour, design, texture, form and function. Children use what they have learnt about media and materials in original ways. Thinking about uses and purposes.

Planning overview: Spring (weeks 5 - 6)

Week	Main topic and activities	ELGs covered from specific areas of learning			
		Literacy including some communication and language	Mathematics	Understanding the world	Expressive arts and design
5	**Spring festivals: Easter, Holi and Mardi Gras** • The Easter story • Pancake maths • Holi traditions • Mardi Gras musical instruments	Sequence the events of the Easter story correctly, retelling it accurately. They answer 'how' and 'why' questions about their experiences and in response to stories or events. Children read and understand simple sentences. They use phonic knowledge to decode regular words and read them aloud accurately. They demonstrate understanding when talking with others about what they have read.	Read, write and use a recipe for pancakes to make enough pancakes for everyone to share! Children count reliably with numbers from 1 to 20, place them in order and say which number is one more or one less than a given number. They solve problems, including doubling, halving and sharing. Children use everyday language to talk about size, weight, capacity, position, distance, time and money to compare quantities and objects and to solve problems.	Look at the festival of Holi and how it is celebrated in other countries. Throw confetti, powder paint or squirt water outdoors. Children talk about past and present events in their own lives and the lives of family members. They know that other children don't always enjoy the same things and are sensitive to this. They know about similarities and differences between themselves and others, and among families, communities and traditions.	Make a musical instrument to play at the Mardi Gras festival parade. Children sing songs, make music and dance and experiment with ways of changing them. They represent their own ideas, thoughts and feelings through design and technology, art, music, dance, role-play and stories.
6	**Sharing with parents and carers**	Spring parade